HUMAN RESOURCES

Volume II

Professional Challenges

Learn the art of leading effective teams.

HUMAN RESOURCES

Volume II Professional Challenges ©

Series: Human Resources

Deluxe Edition – Softcover

Written, illustrated and edited by:

Marbella Yeniree Moya Ochoa

Copyright © 2023

First edition ISBN: 9798865963226

Independent editions

Caracas Venezuela

General Content

DEDICATION 7

FOREWORD... 8

INTRODUCTION 12

CHAPTER I 20

First Secret 20

   Mind Map No. 1.................................... 25

      Your Mind Map No. 1 26

CHAPTER II.. 28

Second Secret 28

   Mind Map No. 2.................................... 33

      Your Mind Map No. 2 34

CHAPTER III... 36

Third Secret 36

   Mind Map No. 3.................................... 41

      Your Mind Map No. 3 42

CHAPTER IV 44

Secret Room 44

   Mind Map No. 4.................................... 51

      Your Mind Map No. 4 52

CHAPTER V 54

Fifth Secret 54

   Mind Map No. 5.................................... 68

      Your Mind Map No. 5 69

CHAPTER VI 71

Sixth Secret 71

  Mind Map No. 6 80

    Your Mind Map No. 6 81

CHAPTER VII 83

Seventh Secret 83

  Mind Map No. 7 94

    Your Mind Map No. 7 95

CHAPTER VIII 97

Eighth Secret 97

  Mind Map No. 8 104

    Your Mind Map No. 8 105

CHAPTER IX 107

Ninth Secret 107

  Mind Map No. 9 119

    Your Mind Map No. 9 120

CHAPTER X 122

Tenth Secret 122

  Mind Map No. 10 129

    Your Mind Map No. 10 130

CHAPTER XI 132

Eleventh Secret 132

  Mind Map No. 11 137

    Your Mind Map No. 11 138

CHAPTER XII 140

Twelfth Secret 140

   Mind Map No. 12 149

     Your Mind Map No. 12 150

REFLECTIONS OF THE AUTHOR 151

WORK NOTEBOOK 160

READER'S REFLECTIONS 167

INTELLECTUAL AUTOBIOGRAPHY 174

BOOKS PUBLISHED ON AMAZON.COM, INC. OR ITS AFFILIATES. 178

DEDICATION

To God and the Blessed Virgin.
To my mother and father Xiomara and Pedro.
To my sisters Mara and Linda.
To my beloved Valeria, Samuel, Santiago,
Miguel, Mateo and my Alfrides Miguel.
My eternal love with you.

FOREWORD

Dear reader, I warmly welcome you to this great book Human Resources and Professional Challenges, where we are going to explore the main secrets that you must strengthen during the twelve months of the year.

We are going to enhance your brilliant mind through the real practice of your skills, because more than secrets that would end up being pure absurd writings, they become real if we practice them with the greatest determination and firmness. You are here reading this book to make a commitment to yourself, because the following pages are going to be a Great Challenge for you.

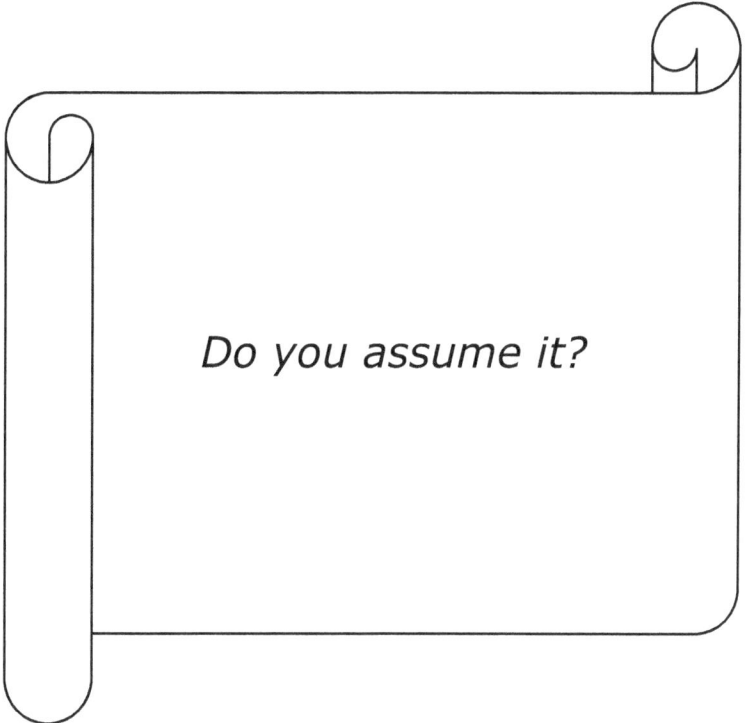

Do you assume it?

If so, keep reading because brilliant minds are the ones that train every day and never defeat themselves.

Skills are trained to the maximum, in a flexible and comprehensive manner; But the most important thing is your commitment to move forward.

The first thing I am going to ask you is that you share everything you learned in this book, with the best comment about this great experience.

I am going to give you some specific techniques to enhance your personal and work well-being, you are going to project yourself with the best of the best and the most important thing is that each secret is 100% practical.

No more excuses for saying this book is a bore and I'm not interested, on the contrary each secret is training for your life, because it is the way you commit to your professional life.

You are going to do these exercises that I am going to put in this book, it is your time, we are going to go through these skills linked to success, in a behavioral, creative and very participatory way.

So welcome again and welcome back to this great challenge of Human Resources and Professional Challenges.

My second book in the Human Resources Series.

Thank you so much for reading me!
THE AUTHOR

INTRODUCTION

Hello, my name is Marbella Yeniree Moya Ochoa and before we start reading this book in great detail I want you to get to know me.

I am president of the Educando para la Paz Foundation and in 2021 alone we reached more than 80,000 people in 124 countries through the continuous training we have in the professional and human field at FEPAZ World Academy, it has been magical, with a job full of love for years, because it all started with citizenship training for children and gradually we created professional training programs, in human talent, in occupational well-being, human well-being.

Strengthening human rights, as a guarantor of that extraordinary human dignity that you have with this book, I come to give you a Great Challenge to present you the best of the best, to have an exponential year.

I am going to give you specific practices so that you can put it in your favor, because the great year of your life has arrived and it all starts with these 12 wonderful practices that I put together in a very detailed way.

I am a political scientist, writer and administrator by profession, graduated from the Central University of Venezuela and also from the Simón Rodríguez National Experimental University in Venezuela, gradually, I continue with many academic training, managing to have more than 13 years of experience and bring you this great challenge together in these 12 professional challenges, in a humane, simple, enjoyable, uncomplicated way.

My methodology is my own, I have brought a supremely bold methodology, always thinking exponentially, that education must break those stereotypes that are of no use to us, thinking exponentially by jumping to the moon, that is, from the earth to the moon , only in this way does education gain that transformation that all human beings need. At this moment we have gone through many things, the last few years have been one of many personal transformations, at a health, emotional, personal level, and what to say about the workplace; So my intention with this book is for you to take it on as a Great Challenge, to take the advantage in your favor.

These 12 secrets, gathered in 12 practices so that you practice them every month of the year, concentrated, just like a pill, the most concentrated, explaining 12 secrets without practicing the 12 months of the year would be throwing everything learned in the trash, for this reason , I detailed a lot of information and gathered the best of the best, researching day and night.

You don't know how many months I have been working on this book, which is undoubtedly a great challenge, because it is not only born with this book, which is the final result; I brought together the best to completely transform your personal and work life as a result of the first book Human Resources Agile Skills in the Series.

I'm going to ask you a big favor for reading this book, comment on social networks and share what you thought of this book.

I wanted to give you much more than a simple book that you read one day and that's it, the pages are closed. It is completely opening your personal and work life transformation through continuous practice. If one day you exercise, you should continue because your brilliant mind is a muscle that always exercises without stopping.

As a mental and physical training, I want to involve you, it is vitally important to know what you think of all this great challenge, and underline it I always challenge you, in all my training courses, in all my books, in everything I do with FEPAZ World Academy and with the Educando para la Paz Foundation – FEPAZ World. And now more with ARH International.

It is putting your mind to work here, breaking the mental molds, leaving your comfort zone and jumping that square that in traditional education always gave us the moment to enliven the leader, the professional, the person who is listening to me; Through this book, revive that great person, that great wonderful human being who lives in you everything to build a better world. So welcome and/or welcome to this great challenge, this great exponential challenge fills me with a lot.

***

HUMAN RESOURCES

Volume II

Professional Challenges

First Secret

FLEXIBILITY

To be applied in the month of JANUARY

CHAPTER I

First Secret

I am going to start now with an essential element to strengthen work well-being in an impactful and forceful way. We begin with flexibility, which is that the pandemic has taught us to leave that rigor and continually adapt to changes.

From this flexibility we are going to mutate the conditions where the doors are opened to us, that is, those traditional jobs "for life", "marrying a job forever"; They were left behind, so one element of flexibility is rotating and expanding. An example of this is, if you have an income, visualize others and enhance them in your favor.

Below I present the first exercise that I propose to increase this flexibility.

The first thing you should always do is take your workbook, pencil and paper at hand, and you will add each of these skills and these exercises that I am going to give you in terms of flexibility.

The second thing is that you take different jobs, other job options, you can have a central one, but try to branch them out, to consult through the internet.

What other options are you going to have to adapt to this?

Look for options, for example the social network Linkedin, check your image first, what you are going to project with these social networks it is vitally important that you have it first hand and start looking there for possible offers that adapt to your profile, explore every week, so that there is not a week left without that intensive search for new jobs.

As I mentioned, if you have a job that pays you well, it is perfect, but look for another that will be complementary.

So these new terms adapt to teleworking in your hours where you do not have that job from 7 to 5 in the afternoon, if you do not have a permanent job, also look for another source of income.

What is necessary to avoid here, in this term of flexibility, is that you take entrepreneurship as a lasting option .

Later I will explain to you about this term but here always be constantly empathetic and with a lot of commitment on your part for that intensive search. As I told you, the pandemic is teaching us to take this ingredient of being flexible, modest to change consecutively, take it as An advantage in your favor, if you put it into practice in your intensive search for other sources of income and opportunities, you will surely have the greatest success.

***

Mind Map No. 1

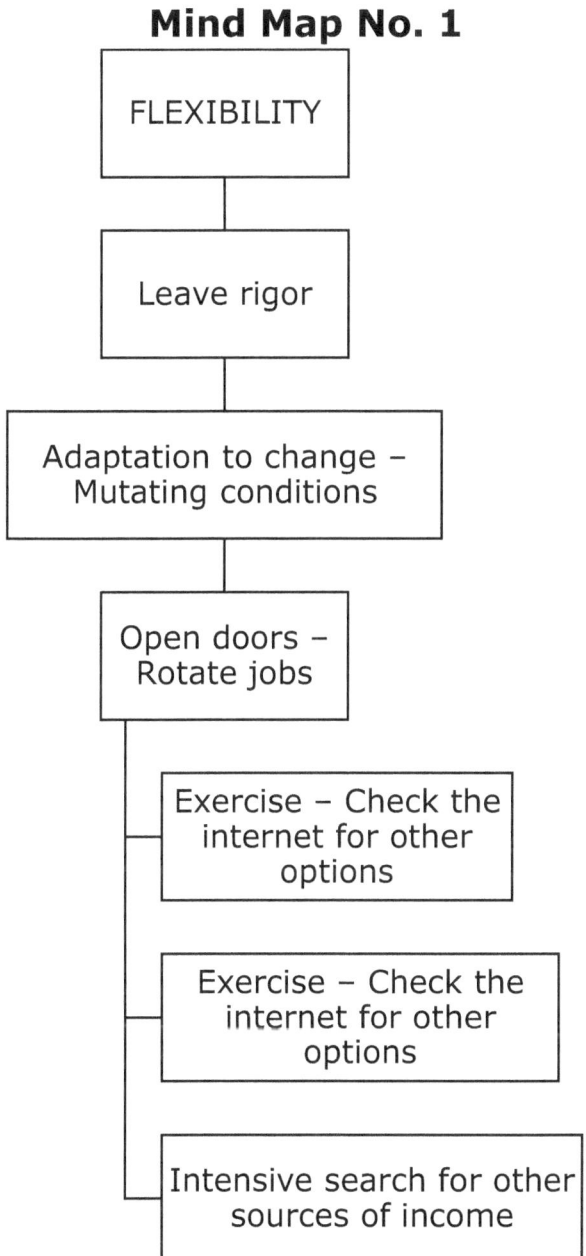

FLEXIBILITY

Leave rigor

Adaptation to change – Mutating conditions

Open doors – Rotate jobs

Exercise – Check the internet for other options

Exercise – Check the internet for other options

Intensive search for other sources of income

Your Mind Map No. 1

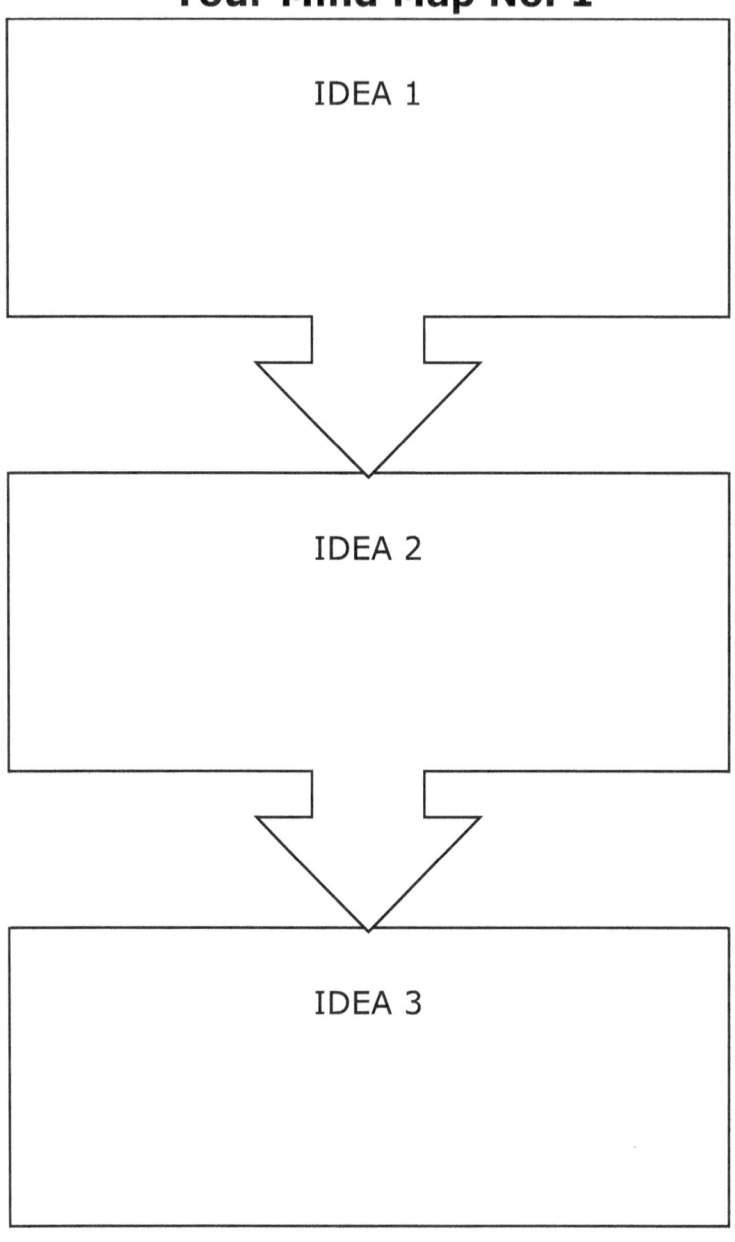

SECOND SECRET

SELF-REGULATION

To be trained in the month of FEBRUARY

CHAPTER II

Second Secret

Emphasizing what was previously stated, these practices are not created overnight, they are not created by themselves.

In a fountain of water that gushes out such knowledge, it is quite the opposite, it takes a lot of focus to be the best professional and part of the leadership that must prevail in you is that although we started with flexibility and now self-regulation, it adds to your life a precept that you must put in your favor.

Knowing that you are going to measure the objectives that you have set, search little by little with that pencil and paper that you will have at any time. Having your own initiative in your workplace, in person, also involves the following.

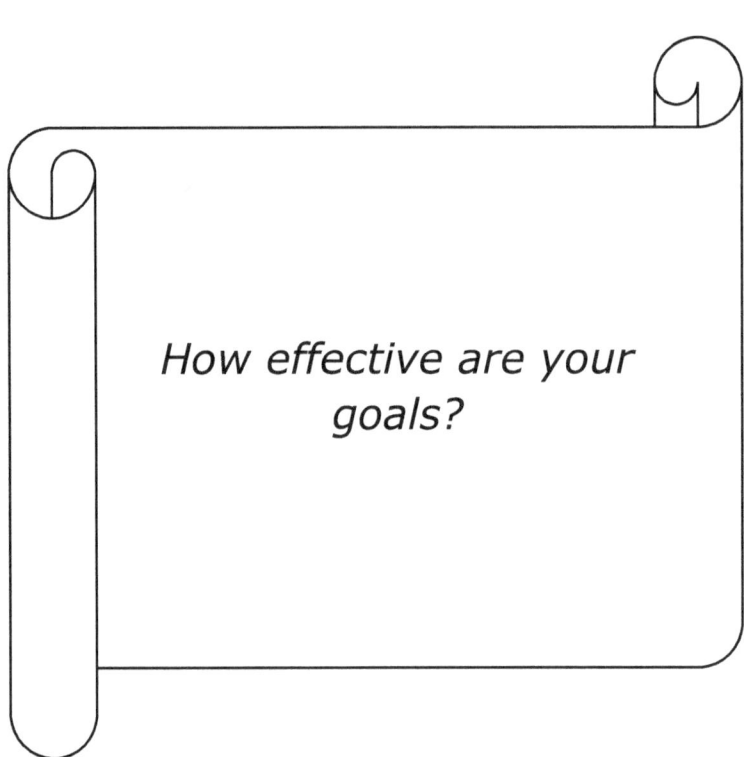

How effective are your goals?

Set short, medium and long-term goals. An example of this is that you are reading this book as a great challenge in your life is that you exercise little by little, just as you did with flexibility, looking for sources of income.

In self-regulation you are going to evaluate the reality that you have today and what you expect and consecutively, it is necessary to look at self-regulation as a self-discipline that you must have in your work life.

The things about job success are the result of feeling fulfilled, like a person who is earning income, who is enjoying success at the level of his life completely; It is not overnight, it is evidence of that self-regulation of measuring certain objectives.

Therefore, you should detail as much as possible what you want to write in pencil and paper, the details cannot go unnoticed. They have to be there. I leave this for you to exercise as a starting point during the month of February. I repeat January with flexibility, February as self-regulation.

***

Mind Map No. 2

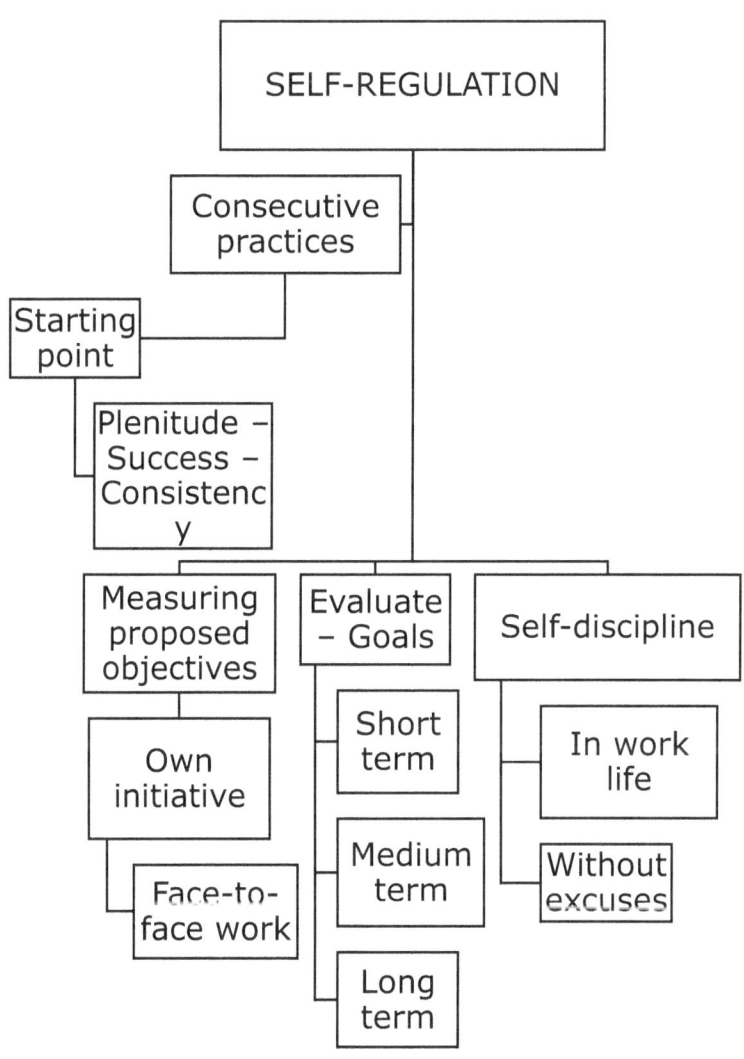

Your Mind Map No. 2

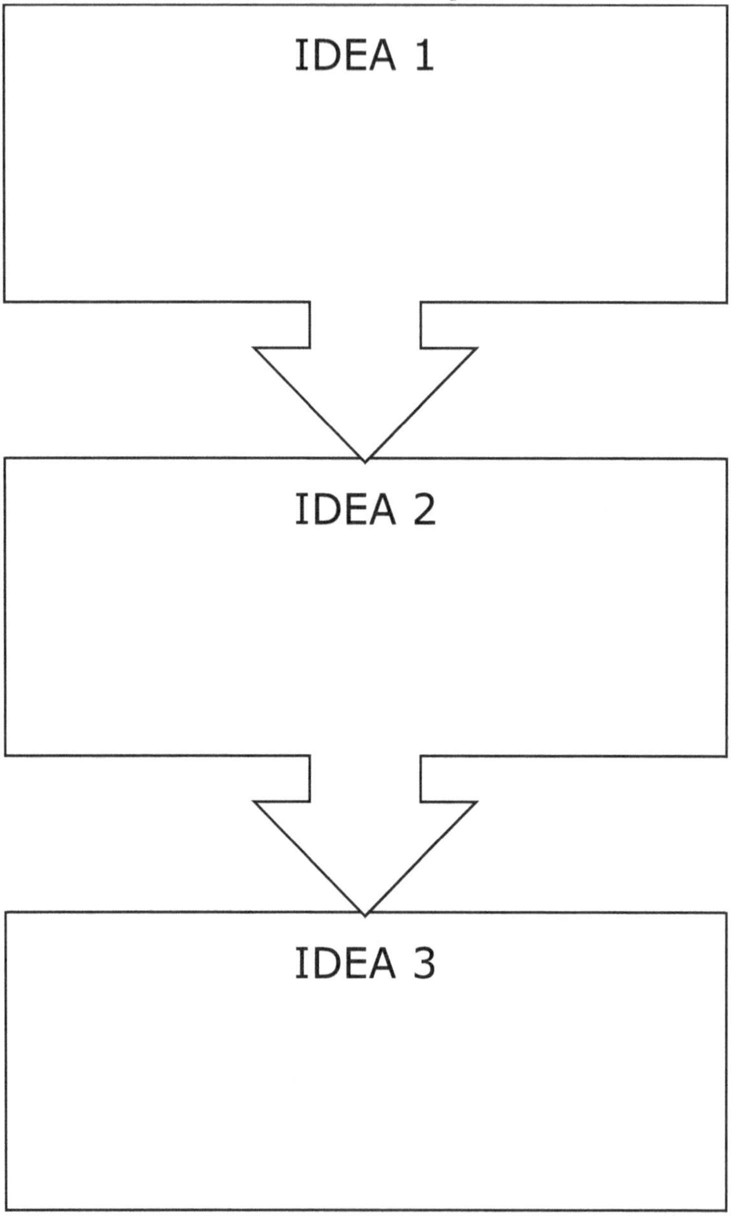

IDEA 1

IDEA 2

IDEA 3

THIRD SECRET

CONTINUOUS LEARNING

To be trained in the month of MARCH

CHAPTER III
Third Secret

You are going to explore new learning, that is, continually get involved in a determined and forceful way in your work life, do not waste any moment and the fact that you are here reading this book is a great challenge for you, because it means that you want to learn, new ways and things at work level.

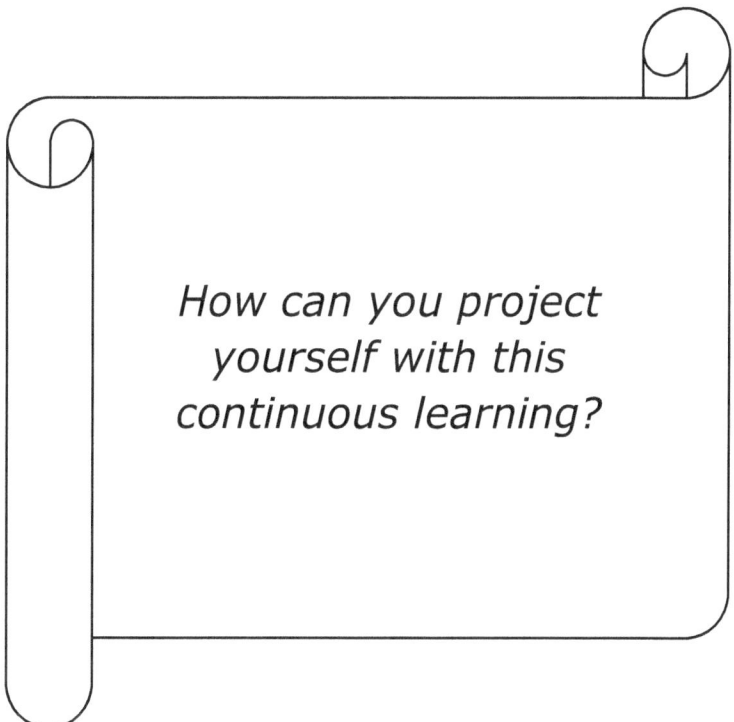

How can you project yourself with this continuous learning?

The answer to this question is through courses, workshops, reading every day, to do so, complement this book with the entire Human Resources Series.

To further project these skills of the great challenge that I am telling you about at that moment, with this continuous learning also take pencil and paper.

Next, seek to learn new ways, for example, if you are a lawyer, seek to learn other things that can nourish you, do not stay only in legal terms but other disciplines that nourish your professional development. One of these is the area of technology, which I put as a motivator for all careers, it is an area that should be applied to everyone equally, just as health is also, if you read throughout the

Resources Series Humans, revolves around many things applied in the area of workplace well-being and here this new knowledge will bring you greater professional consolidation.

Not only a curriculum vitae, a resume, whatever you want to call it, but that whole panorama of possibilities and what I mentioned before, of looking for new ventures, self-employment and looking for new options.

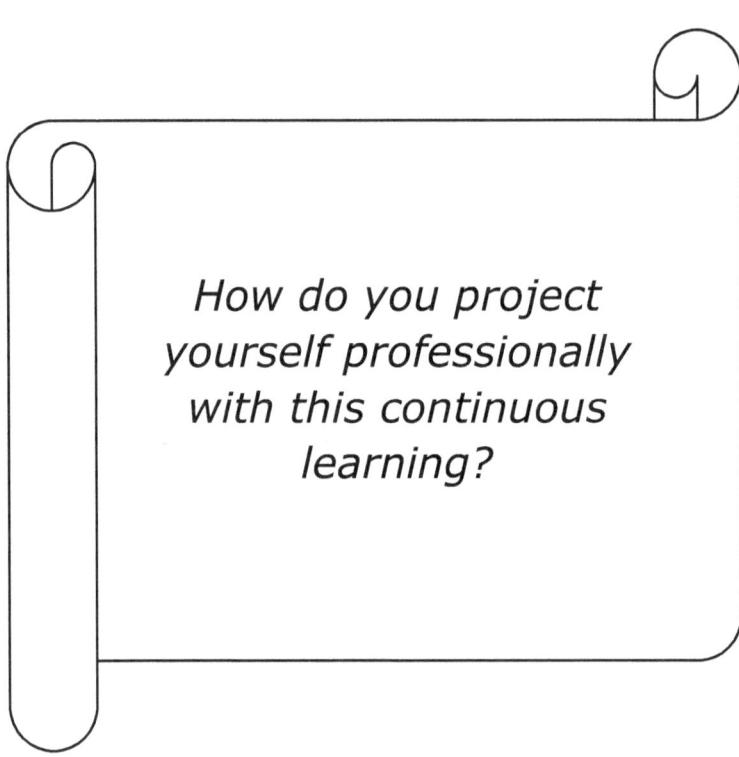

How do you project
yourself professionally
with this continuous
learning?

***

Mind Map No. 3

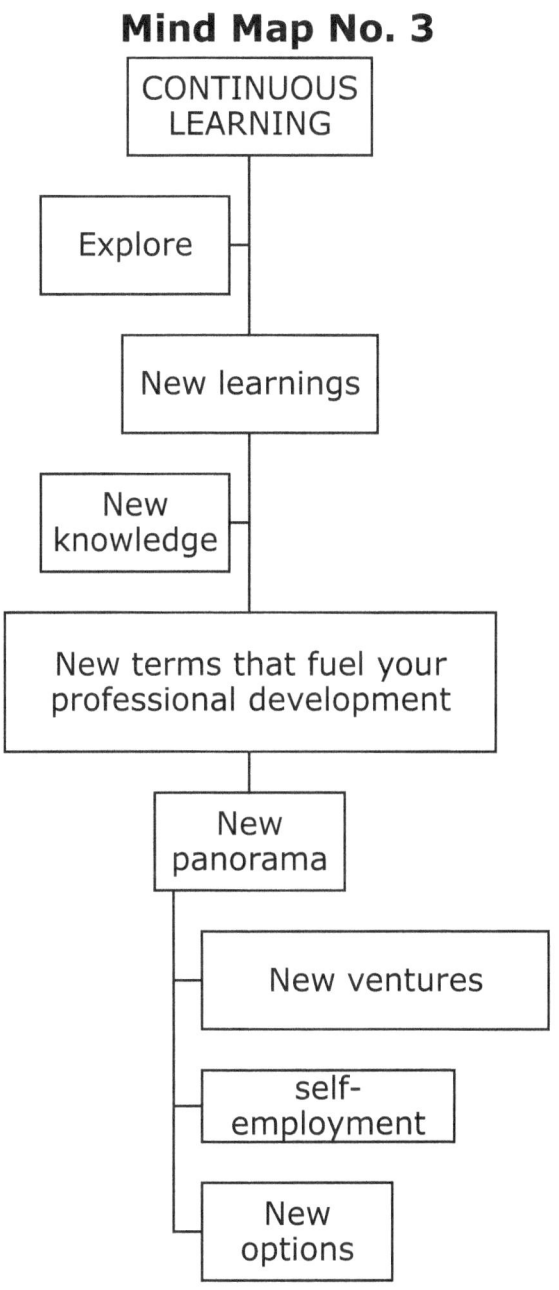

CONTINUOUS LEARNING

Explore

New learnings

New knowledge

New terms that fuel your professional development

New panorama

New ventures

self-employment

New options

Your Mind Map No. 3

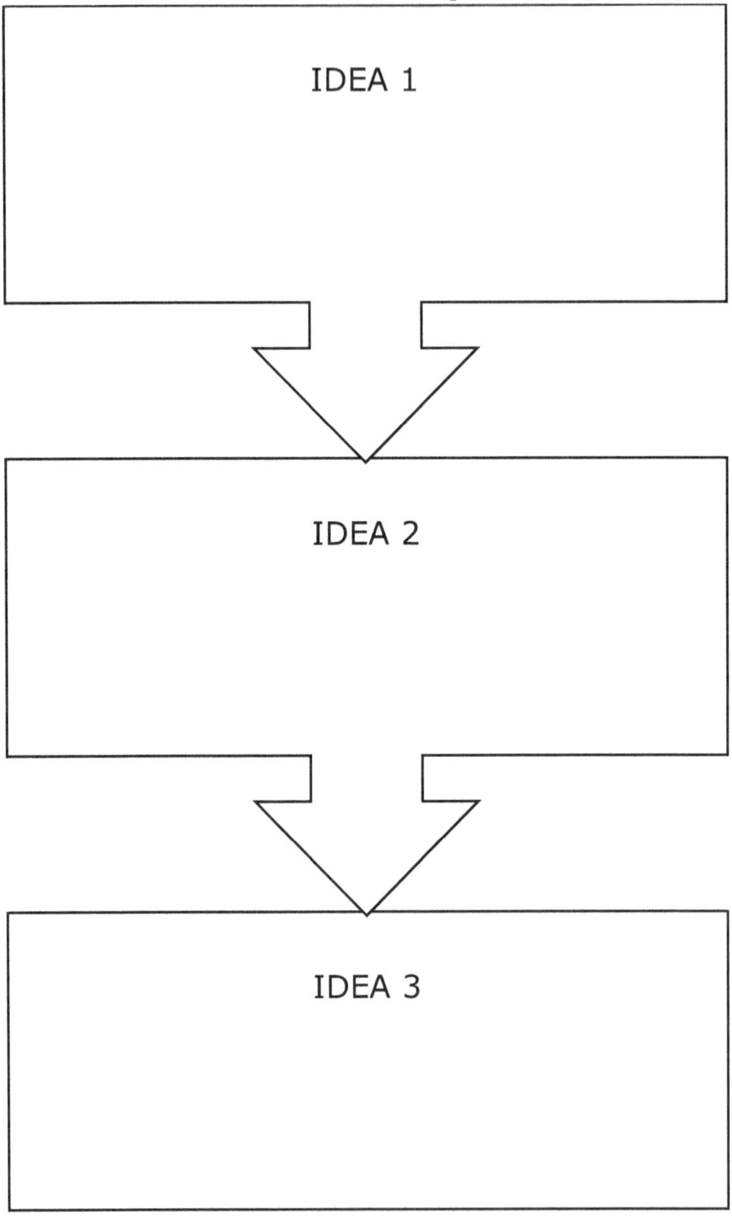

IDEA 1

IDEA 2

IDEA 3

SECRET FOURTH

TEAMWORK

To be trained in the month of APRIL

CHAPTER IV
Fourth Secret

Here the most important thing is that you begin to see that the way of isolating yourself is not an option, you should not isolate yourself as a life option at a work level, you must always work as a team, although you can be a freelancer, self-employed worker, although you may be an entrepreneur, always work as a team and strengthening relationships with other people can help you give those references that you should have in your personal and work life.

Projecting allows you to grab information from other people that can nourish what you are saying and doing.

You are going to make it a constant practice to look for the most educated people next to you and verify the opinions they have regarding new employment possibilities.

What references can they give you?

What are your jobs like?

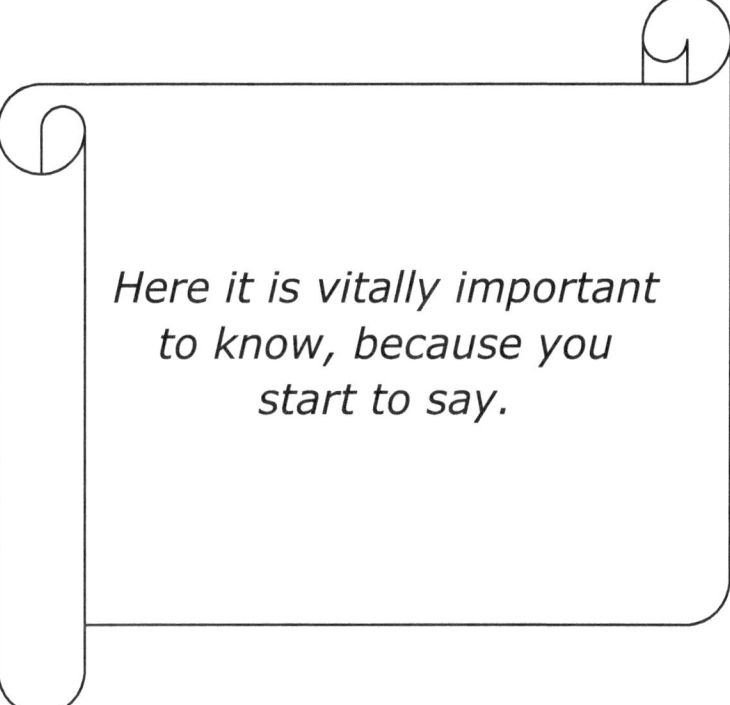

Here it is vitally important to know, because you start to say.

"If this person is working this way, I prefer to have a much calmer, heavier, more harmonious job."

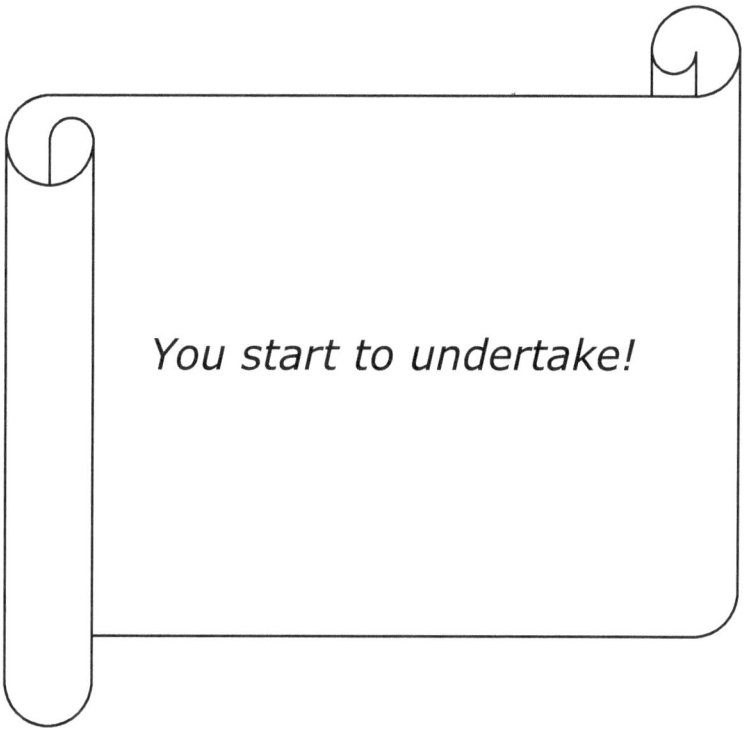

You start to undertake!

As I tell you, this is a fundamental premise during the great challenge that you have assumed with the advantage in your favor, with this teamwork, because it can be collaborative.

For example: If a person is in an excellent job, they can recommend you, if a person is starting a business, you can sell them your own products, so take it as this feedback, this exchange of ideas and goods, services or products, becomes your own professional magnet to project yourself towards lasting well-being with this great annual challenge.

***

Mind Map No. 4

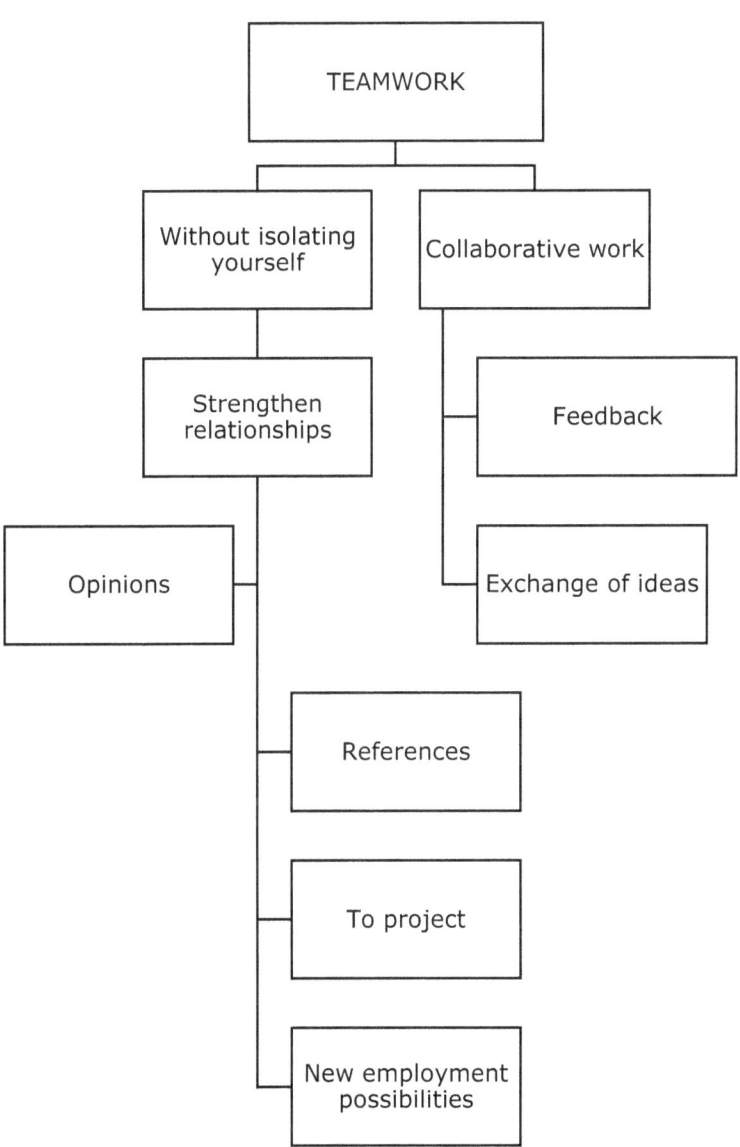

IDEA 1

IDEA 2

IDEA 3

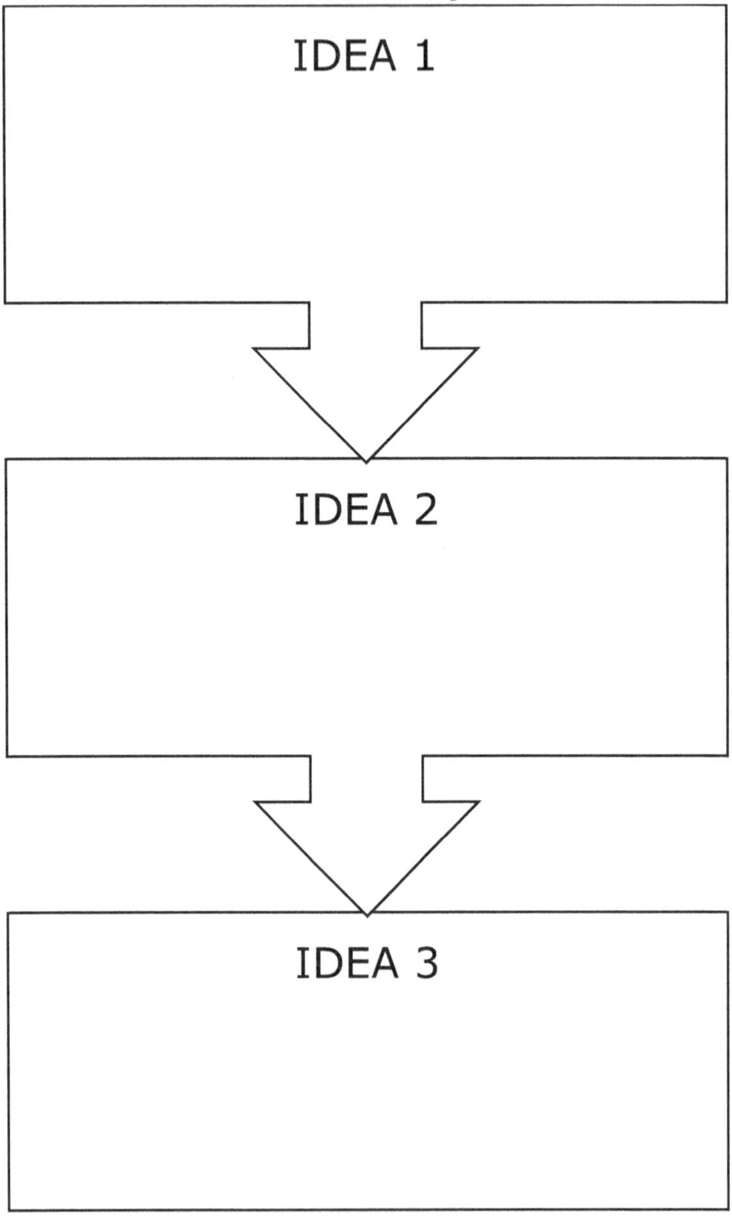

FIFTH SECRET

WITH RESULTS ORIENTATION

To be trained in the month of MAY

CHAPTER V
Fifth Secret

Planning comes to life to give results. Because planning continuously, every month, is essential.

A year without planning is destined for guaranteed failure and I can tell you, because I am a mentor, you follow me throughout this book, throughout my courses and my social networks, you see that I always try to guide you towards that quality of life that you deserve, planning is what will give you that safe path.

As if seeing my results, my work life in perfect order.

In January, you started with flexibility, in February, March, April; We are in May of planning.

How do you orient
yourself?

Check out

How does this planning
impact your life?

We are not halfway through the year yet so this fifth month is beginning to show.

How is the transmission of all this knowledge that you are learning?

Are you being flexible?

How is your results orientation in May?

If you have managed to meet the objectives you set for yourself in the month of January.

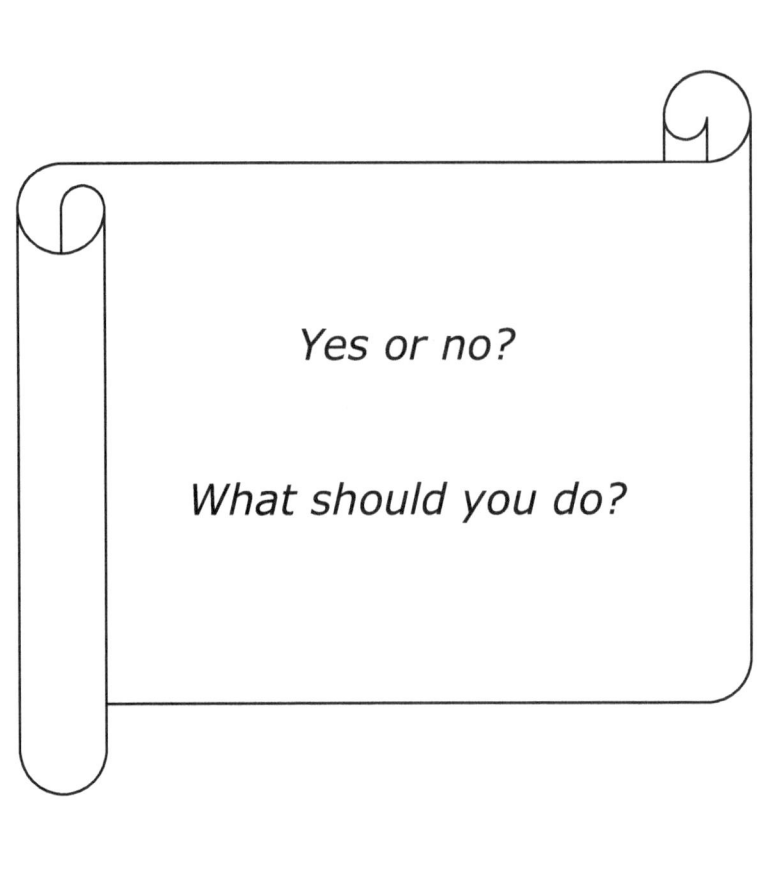

Yes or no?

What should you do?

That will depend exclusively on you, what you should do to achieve them and if not modify them, to be calm and not build rafts and rafts of failures, because it is good that a failure can help you understand the following.

What does success look like?

But, what makes us prevent these triumphs are the continuous failures, abandoning what we have started, so my invitation is that we stop suffering, we did not come into the world to be unhappy, if you have suffered internally, then my invitation to see beyond .

We came to be happy!

So in this results orientation the key is to be more efficient, through planning, this is a date with this secret "planning" in this month of May.

Planning exponentially in a forceful and determined detailed manner!

With pencil and paper at hand, write down your objectives and if you are not achieving them, it is time to modify them and add others that are measurable and achievable, in the short term, you check if you achieved them, then in the medium term, you verify what you have achieved. You reached it and in the long term you do the same thing again.

Mind Map No. 5

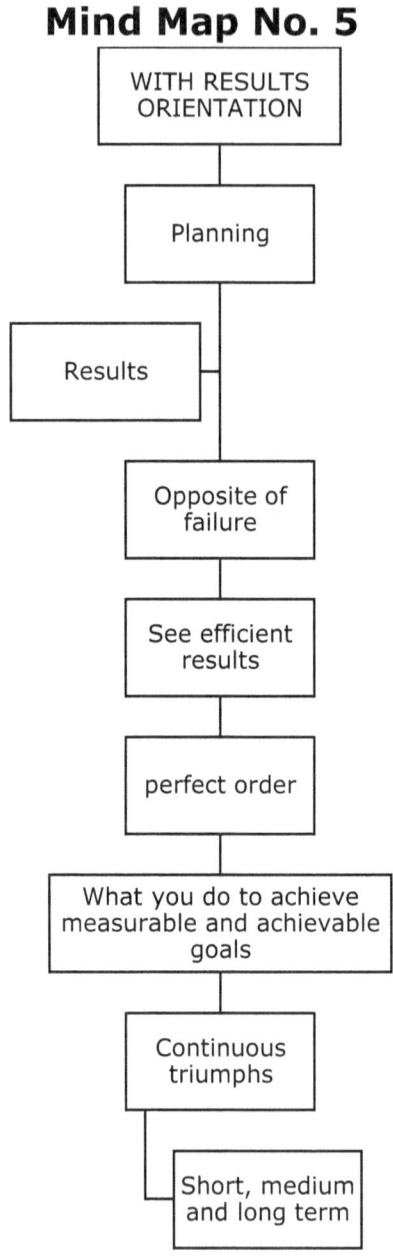

WITH RESULTS ORIENTATION

Planning

Results

Opposite of failure

See efficient results

perfect order

What you do to achieve measurable and achievable goals

Continuous triumphs

Short, medium and long term

Your Mind Map No. 5

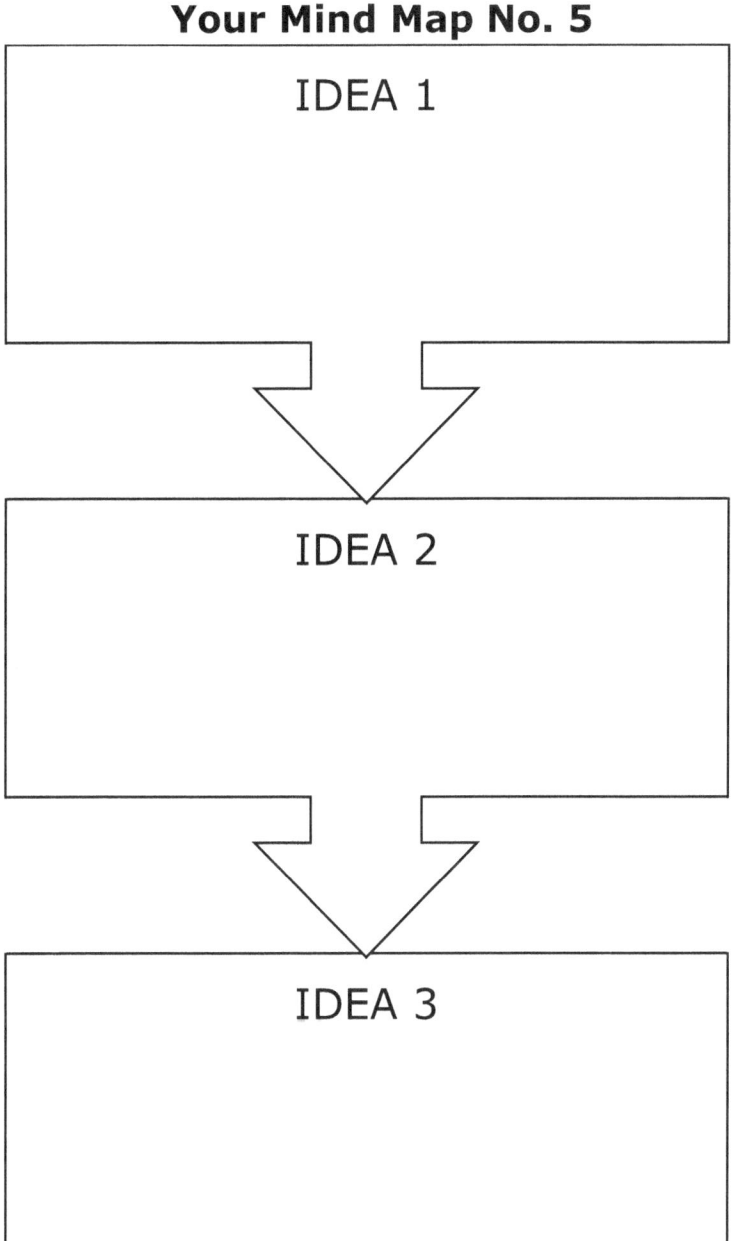

SIXTH SECRET

EMOTION MANAGEMENT

To be trained in the month of JUNE

CHAPTER VI
Sixth Secret

In this world without emotional management we are condemned to repeat the vicious circle of failures, disappointments and continuous frustrations.

Although in January we begin a year to heal ourselves from the soul, it is also true that almost halfway through the year, which is June, you are going to start reviewing again.

How are your emotions?

How do you handle them?

So avoid everything that is not important, here resilience, emotional intelligence, is key, but also that cognitive intelligence that must be in your favor to avoid issues of poor health, stress, depression and mistreatment of others as well, Due to decisions that are not so correct in this management of emotions, you are going to start doing this practice that I mention below.

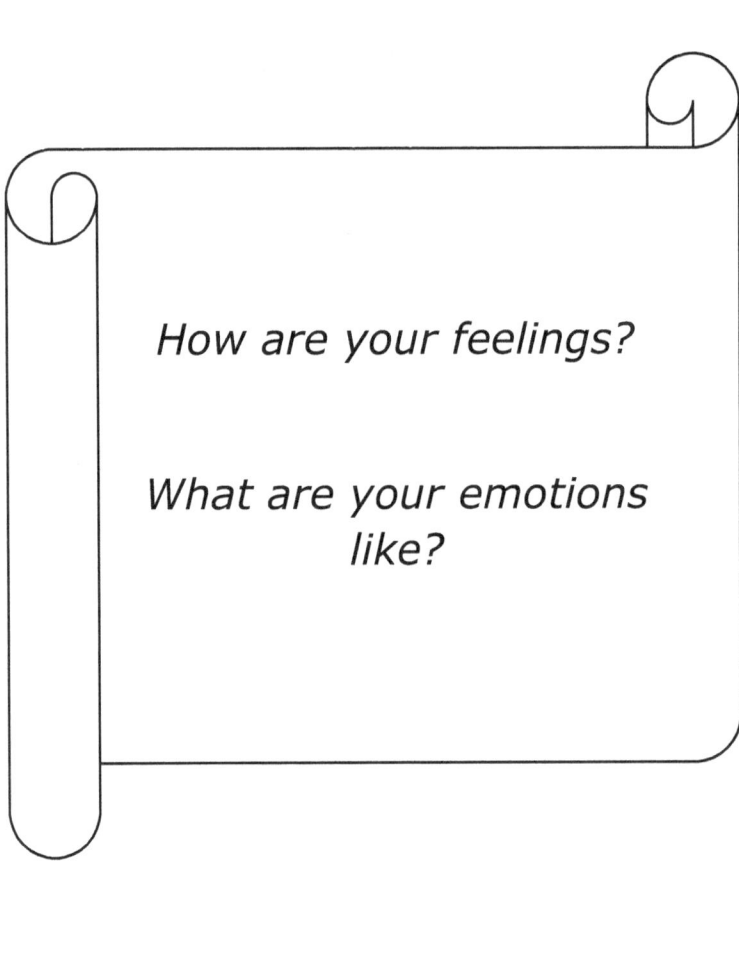

How are your feelings?

What are your emotions like?

Here you start reviewing what happened in May, because guiding the results does not work without this management of emotions; For example, you can't talk if you're depressed.

In the middle of the year, managing those emotions rationally is essential, but also applying your heart, so you need to see how you feel in June.

Review and take notes in the workbook at the back of the book.

*How much are you aware
of your emotions on a
daily basis?*

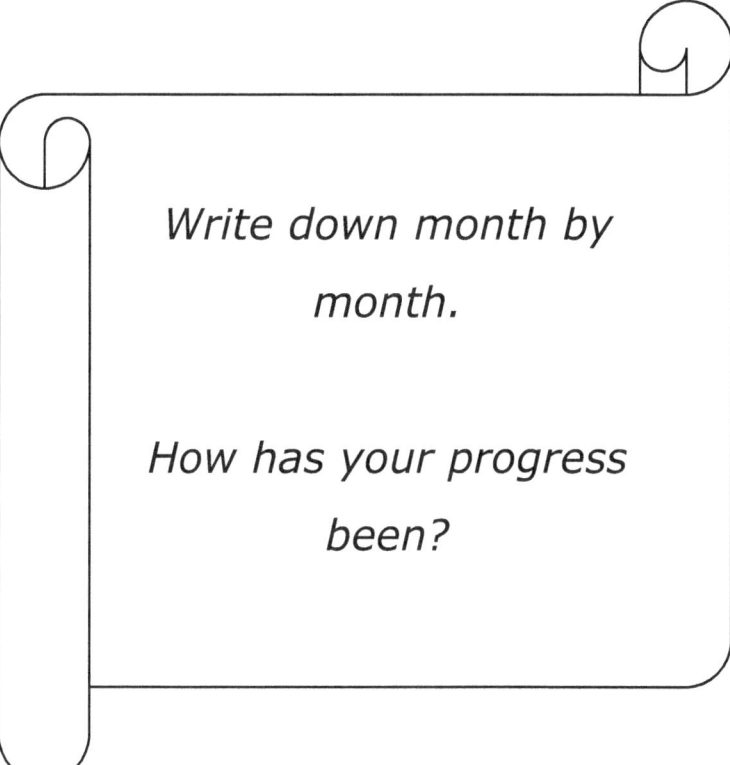

Write down month by month.

How has your progress been?

If there is something that bothers you at the moment, relieve your heart, only so that all that learning and all that adaptation change that you are experiencing in your life can fully occur.

That the moment to be flexible with these emotions you also have to be flexible, to learn that many of them must be valued from the understanding and understanding for yourself, if there are things that you are going through in your life, whether positive or negative as you want to see them; It is time to review them to be grateful for what you are going through and let go.

At this moment you have reached June perfecting every moment of your personal and work life and you are growing without stopping to cry, because it is more important and in this June challenge; see the management of emotions, from the heart and mind, to project and take action to correct the emotions when necessary for your well-being.

Mind Map No. 6

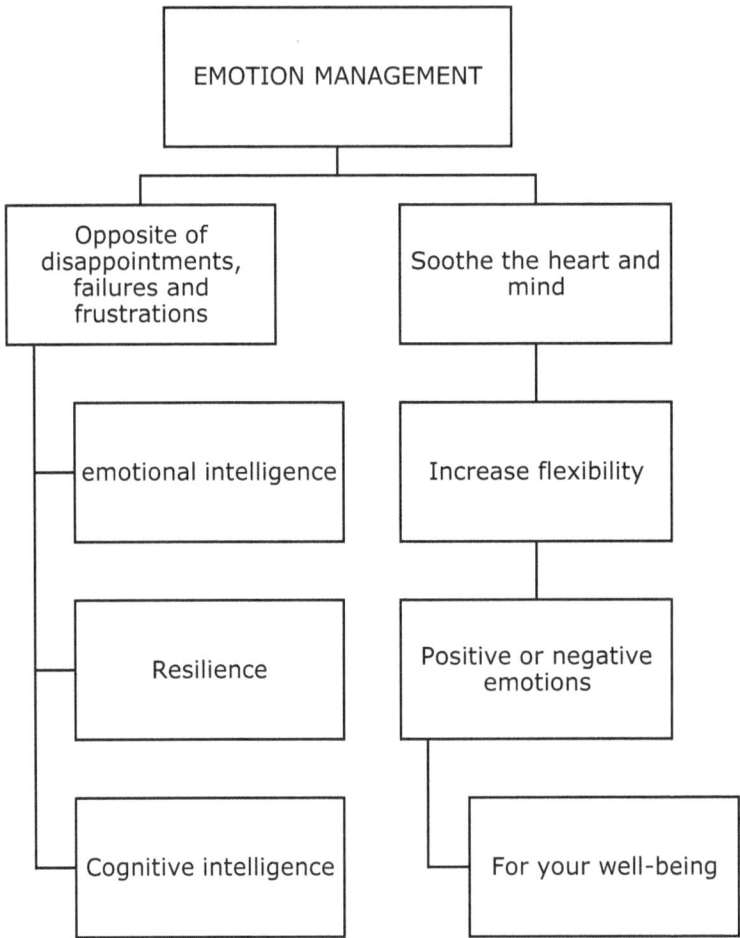

Your Mind Map No. 6

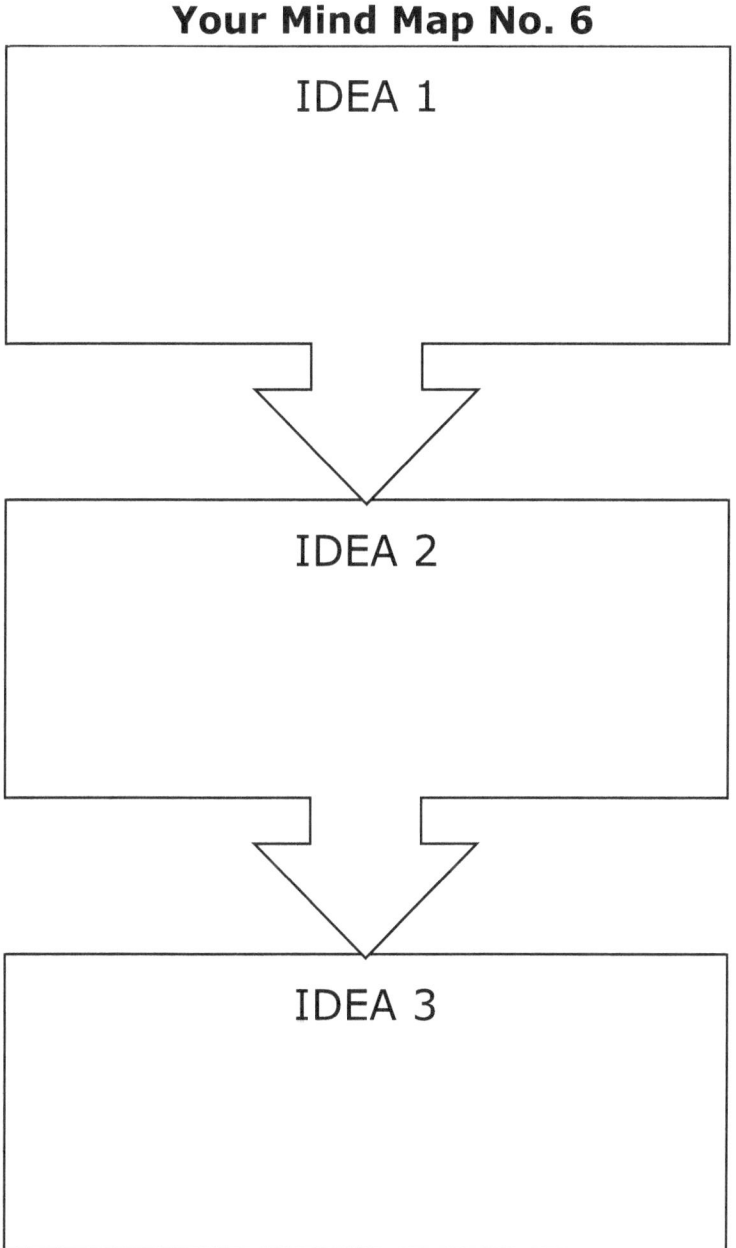

SEVENTH SECRET

ASSERTIVE COMMUNICATION

To be trained in the month of JULY

CHAPTER VII
Seventh Secret

We start with assertive communication, which you will have to exercise every day. It is a great challenge for you, because if you have stage fright, it is difficult for you to speak in public and you don't know how.

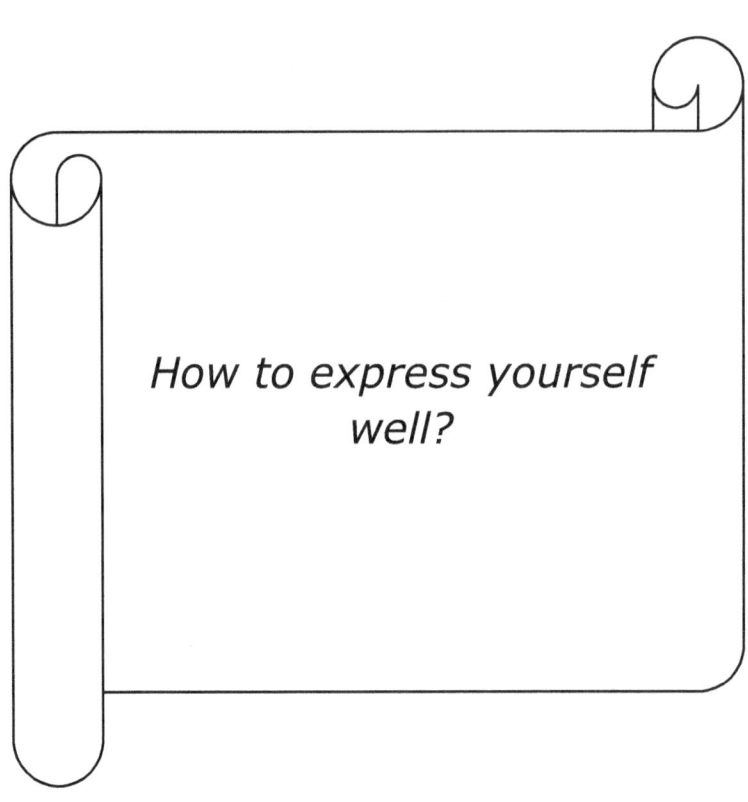

How to express yourself well?

This month you have to be dedicated exclusively to strengthening your assertive communication in an efficient and effective way, so that you project them to the maximum.

Put this in your favor because it is a quality that is being well paid in jobs and is one of the most in-demand skills during the pandemic and post-pandemic, so start doing assertive communication exercises.

An example here and I also share it in my courses and the Human Resources Series, this time you are not going to take a pencil and paper, but grab your cell phone and you will record a video introducing yourself, it starts with just you.

In a room, where you feel comfortable, you will begin to record a personal presentation, here is a challenge that I put it this way, clear and forceful.

How do you present yourself to others, to executives, to a company?

How do you project yourself?

Do you smile?

If you don't know, it's okay, you admit it and if you're afraid to record, it's time to break up if you're afraid of a camera.

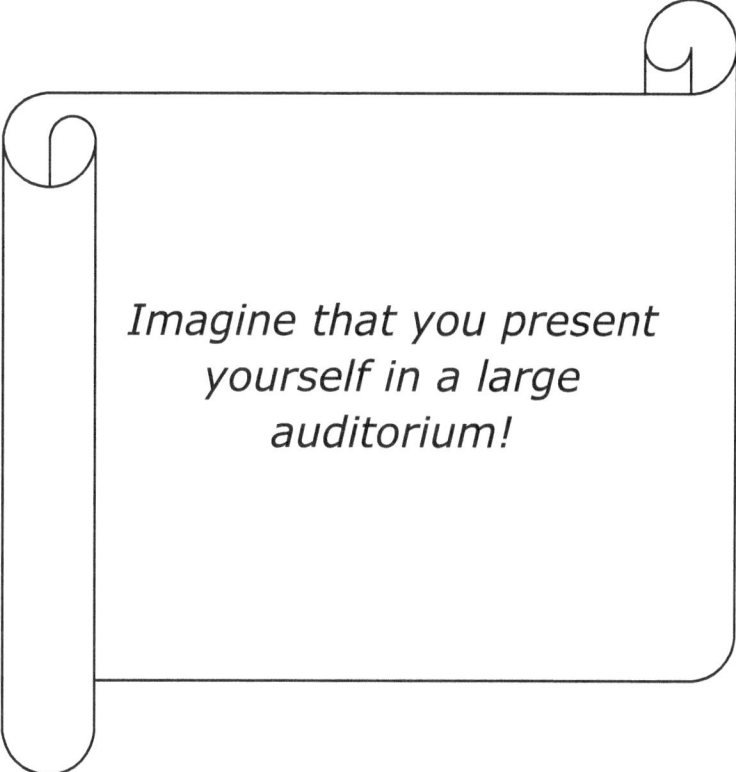

Imagine that you present yourself in a large auditorium!

It would be fatal so my intention with this challenge is for you to develop much more, to win it, you will have to take the reins of your assertive communication, the first recording can be fatal but the second will be better and the third super great.

Thus, the practice of assertive and effective communication, you are going to do it every day, a day that you don't do it, is a day that you go back; Communication was made to train it, no matter what limitations you have, put it in your favor, because I am 100% sure that it is what is going to give you that projection of work well-being and excellent professional.

We have come with flexibility, results orientation, self-regulation, management of your emotions, they come to life here with this effective communication because once you know that you manage your emotions well, that you project yourself without depression, without stress, free from those diseases or bad habits you may have.

With this communication you project the leader in you and that leadership, that good worker, becomes a totally confident entrepreneur to be overwhelming in everything he does.

So put it in your favor by recording, exposing your opinion to other people.

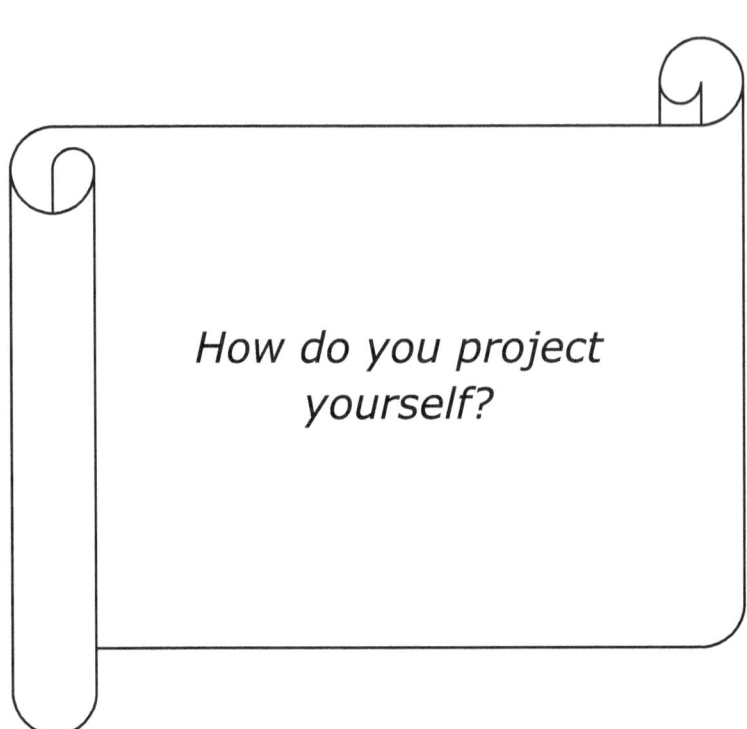

How do you project
yourself?

*Always with a nice smile
that projects the great
professional you are!*

***

Mind Map No. 7

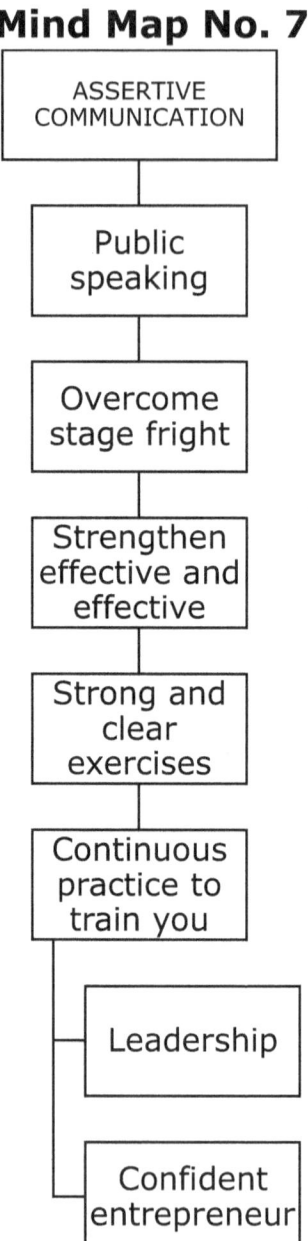

ASSERTIVE COMMUNICATION

Public speaking

Overcome stage fright

Strengthen effective and effective

Strong and clear exercises

Continuous practice to train you

Leadership

Confident entrepreneur

Your Mind Map No. 7

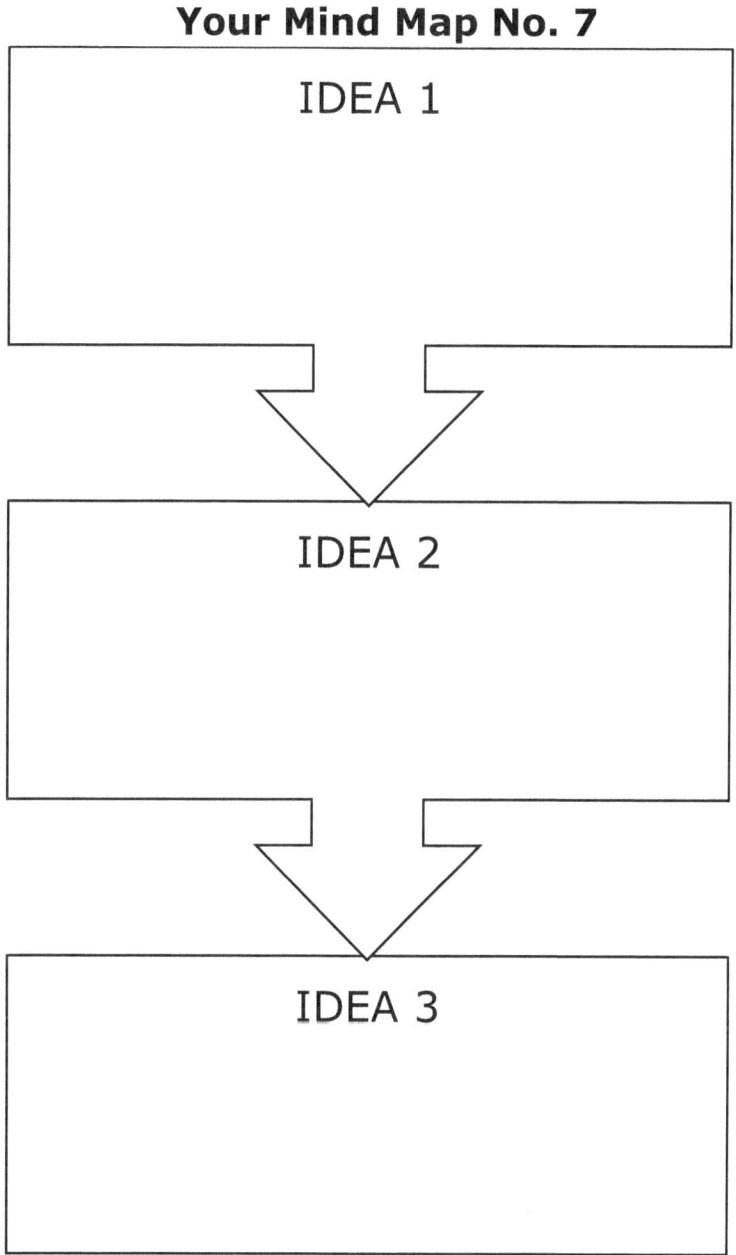

EIGHTH SECRET

ART THERAPY

To be trained in the month of AUGUST

CHAPTER VIII
Eighth Secret

This month the great challenge that I propose to you is through creativity and imagination, so whether there is an artist within you or not during August, you need to put it to exercise. You will create something that is born in you through art therapy.

It is a tool that all professionals should have in their lives, anyone, even as children, should apply it to our lives, because it is what will heal us in the face of any adversity that comes our way.

Art therapy consists of letting our imagination carry away through painting, through art. You don't necessarily have to be a great artist or a great facilitator of these Fine Arts, here you have to grab a notebook whatever you want and create freely.

Getting creative with pencils, colors, markers, acrylics, letting your imagination fly, is a way to release stress, it goes hand in hand with managing emotions, but here it adds up because in a skill that if you practice it. It adds positive value, it helps you visualize what you want.

I propose to you, set the objectives you have, review them again through this creativity and imagination that during the month of August you should continue exploring this practice.

Necessarily, be applied at least once every week, that is, every Monday or every Friday of the month of August; Mostly if it is possible to do it once every day for 5 minutes, make a stroke as you want, it doesn't matter if it is just the old fashioned way, with a pen, a single color or multicolored.

The idea is that you encourage creativity through the canvases that you begin to create. If you don't like it, take it as a moment to learn something unexplored, that you didn't have the knowledge of, and you are going to add the music of your choice while you draw. While doing art therapy, play music that you like to relax, so that you feel much more satisfied.

You've already passed the middle of the year and you're starting to see again.

Take it as this recreational stage where you are going to revive your ideas.

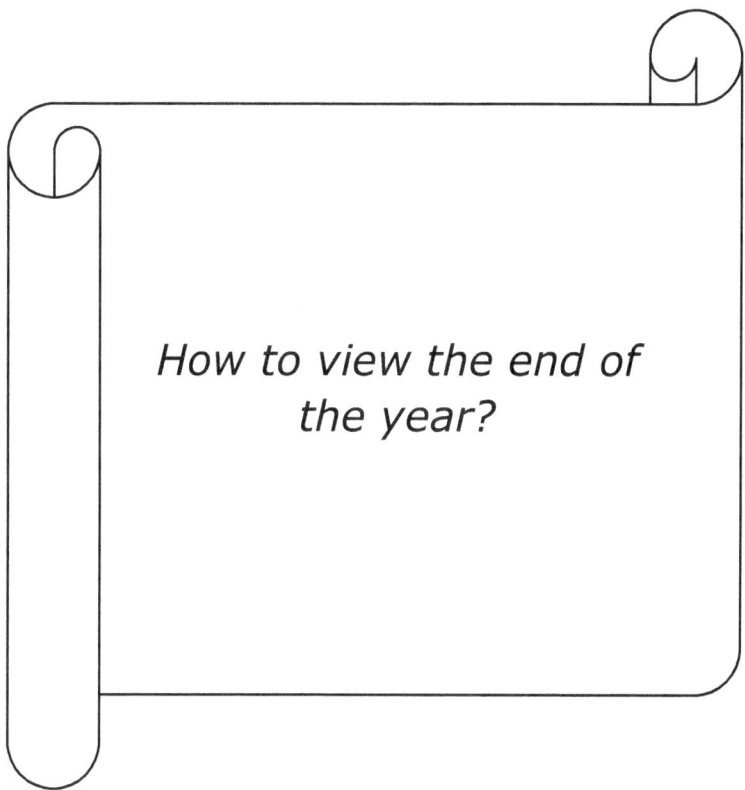

How to view the end of the year?

What did you happen?

How did it happen to you?

What can you improve?

In this art therapy exercise, the most appropriate thing is that you project through this everything that is repressed, the positive experiences that you have lived are also reflected; because it releases all the burdens that one can have and it is very gratifying when you see the final result on a canvas.

Art is a lot of imagination and anything goes, so I leave you this challenge since August with a lot of creativity and imagination through art therapy.

***

Mind Map No. 8

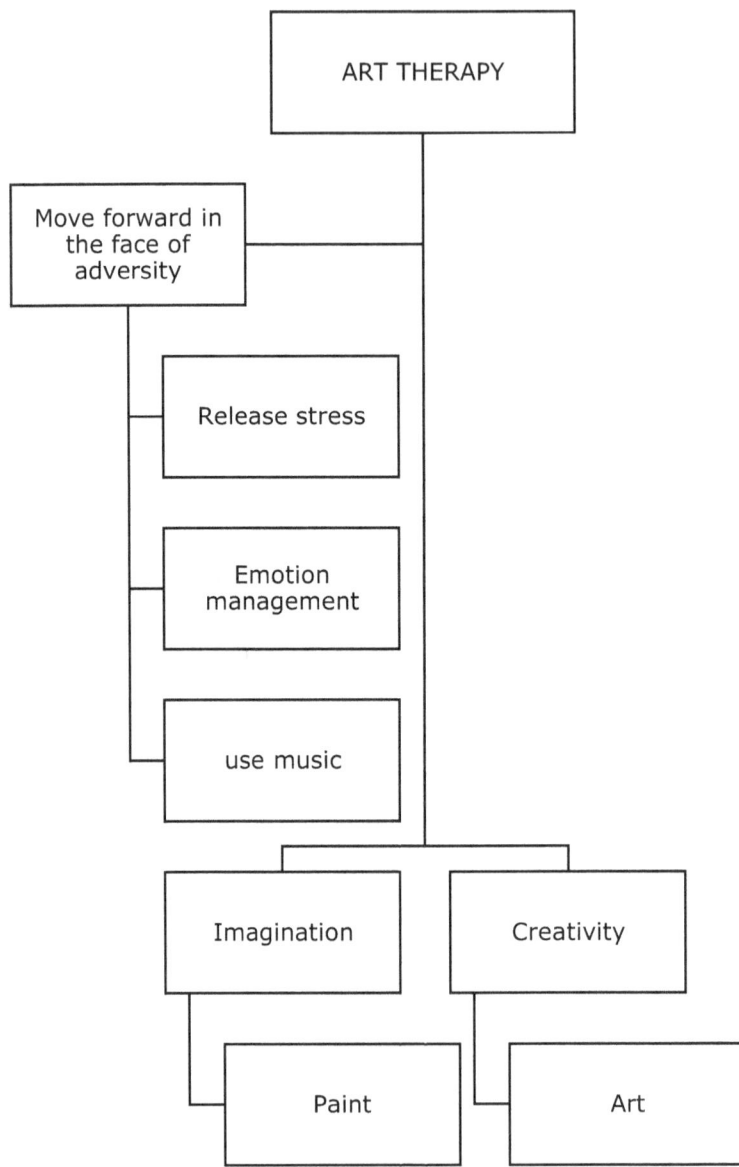

ART THERAPY

Move forward in the face of adversity

Release stress

Emotion management

use music

Imagination

Creativity

Paint

Art

Your Mind Map No. 8

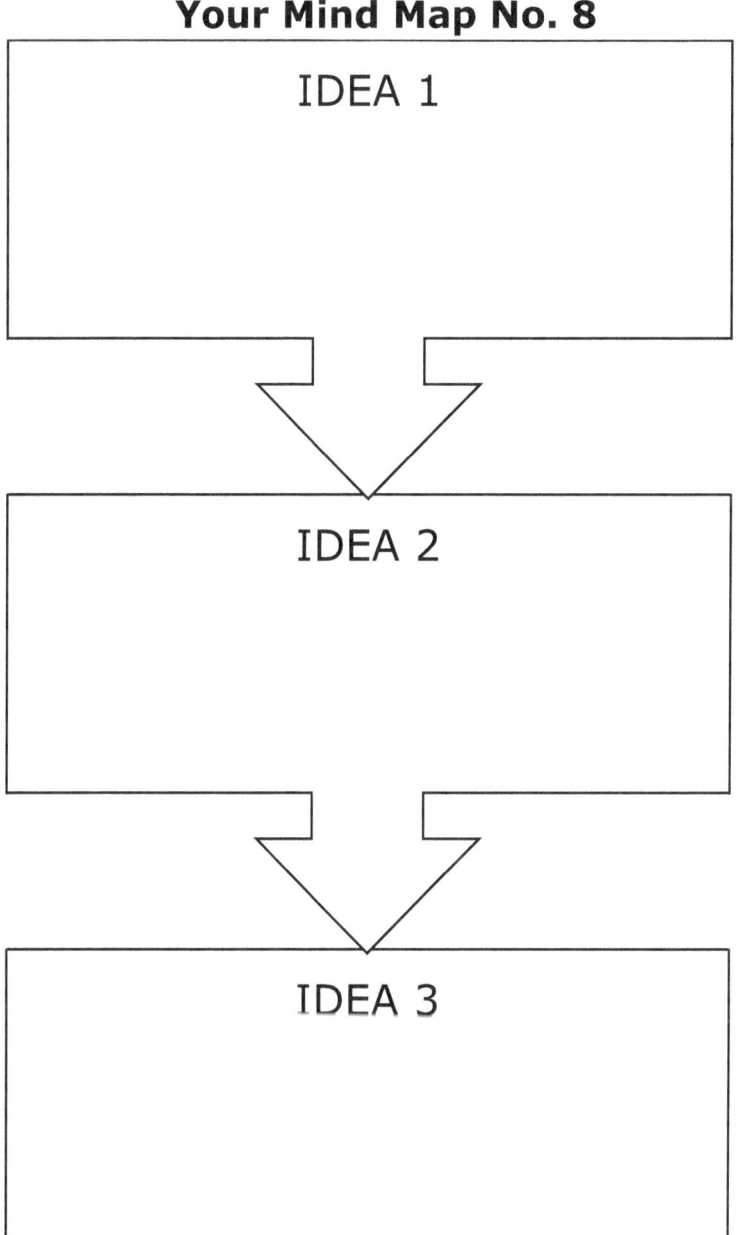

NINTH SECRET

TECHNICAL AND PROFESSIONAL KNOWLEDGE FOR A GOOD INCOME

To be trained in the month of SEPTEMBER

CHAPTER IX
Ninth Secret

After all these months with this great challenge, we have been strengthening ourselves to be forceful and talk about the technical part.

What technical and professional knowledge have you acquired?

How are you dealing with them in your professional life, in your work life?

How is it projecting you?

What did you learn in your life?

What new knowledge do you have?

If there is something physical, a course that you have taken and that you already have a cardboard, something concrete with this technical knowledge. It goes hand in hand with technology, seeing how we can project ourselves through it.

Grab the pencil and paper again and tell your ideas in a video, compare the before and after.

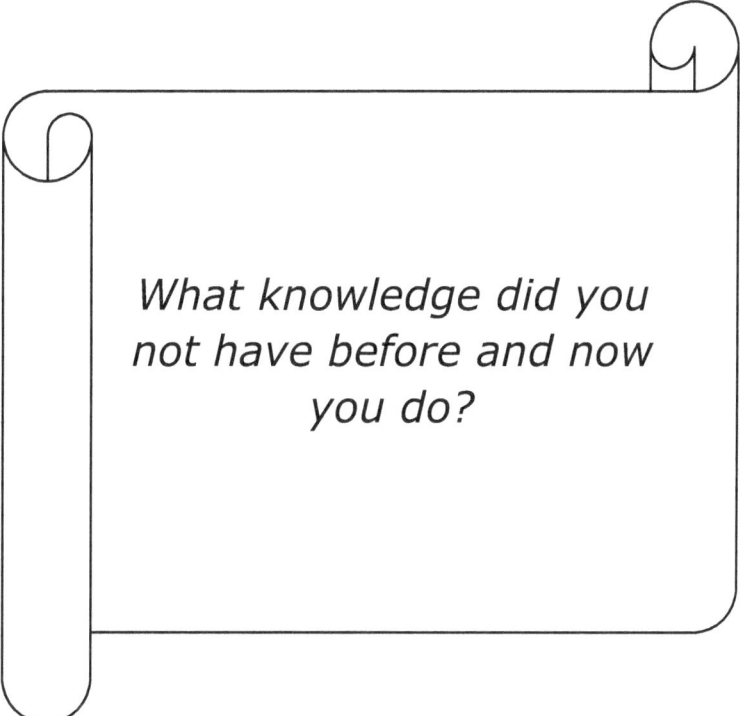

What knowledge did you not have before and now you do?

In the month of September you now have the time to see in an expansive way this technical professional knowledge, the new thing you have done, which is reflected on a cardboard, on a wall, in a new job, in a new quality of life, that you have improved from all these exercises.

How do you feel in the month of September?

With these professional skills that you have been adding, new books, knowledge, practices that you didn't know about. For example, I did not do art therapy, but now it has helped me to be more flexible because before I had only one job, now I have two, now I have a business that I started with great determination and discipline applying all this technical and professional knowledge that I did not assume before. .

You begin to know the importance of planning, which speaks to you in the previous months, like in September you review it again and results are evident.

If you have achieved your goals

Why haven't you achieved them?

One of the important aspects is that you do not judge yourself, do not give yourself the whip of self-punishment, it is time to say the following.

I stop, check and move on!

Project from this technical-professional knowledge that you have, you have added it and you have paid attention to the other months, it is time to review because the year has not yet ended to strengthen this great challenge.

***

Mind Map No. 9

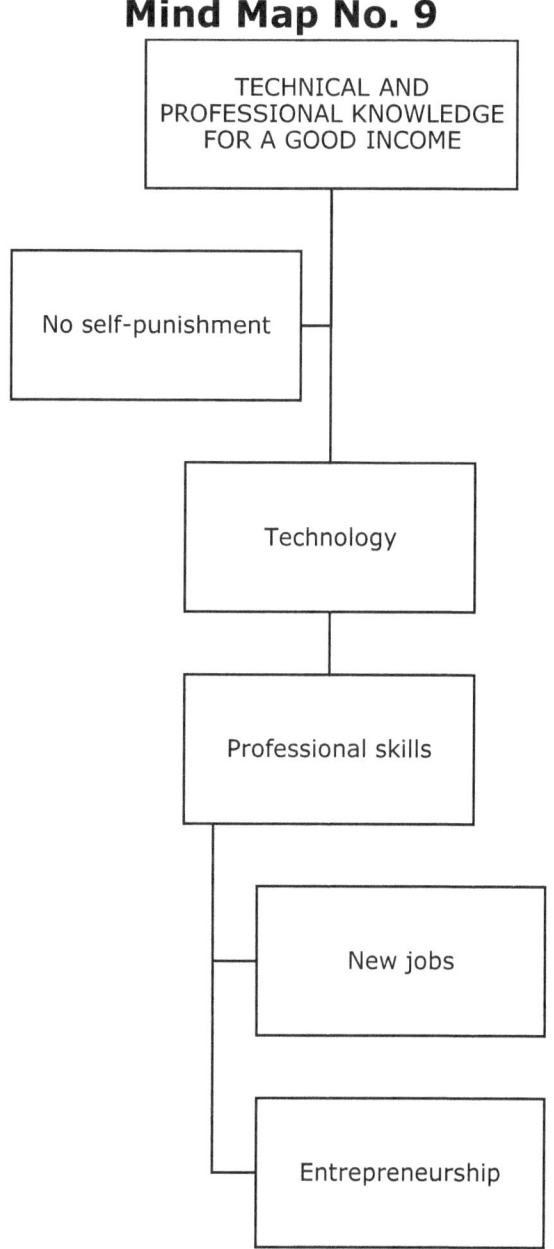

TECHNICAL AND PROFESSIONAL KNOWLEDGE FOR A GOOD INCOME

No self-punishment

Technology

Professional skills

New jobs

Entrepreneurship

Your Mind Map No. 9

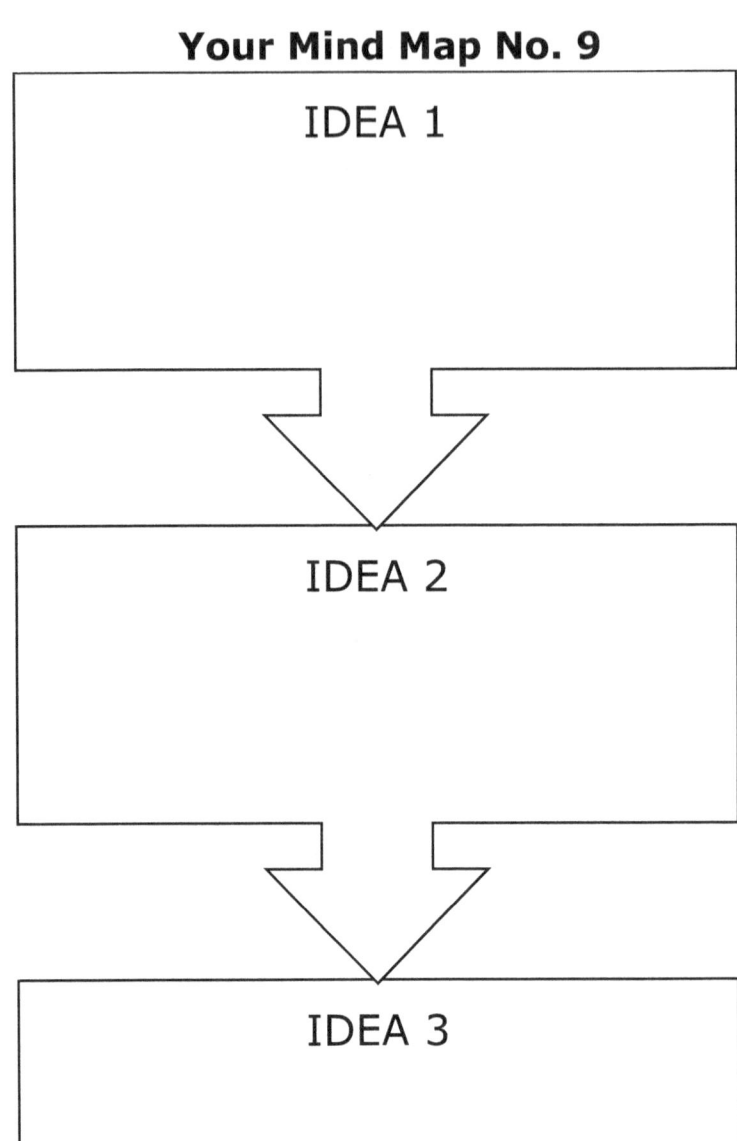

TENTH SECRET

MORE INCOME

To be trained in the month of OCTOBER

CHAPTER X
Tenth Secret

We had already been working on entrepreneurship with new sources of employment and the form of self-employment.

How do you offer your services?

What are your professional projects like?

In October you will have new income, adding to the end of the investments, you will learn about new forms of employment but through the investments you can make, it is necessary that you train yourself in investments; Do not invest overnight with anyone who tells you, train yourself continuously, that is why I was talking about training in knowledge.

In October, it hasn't reached December, it's time to get going if you haven't done so.

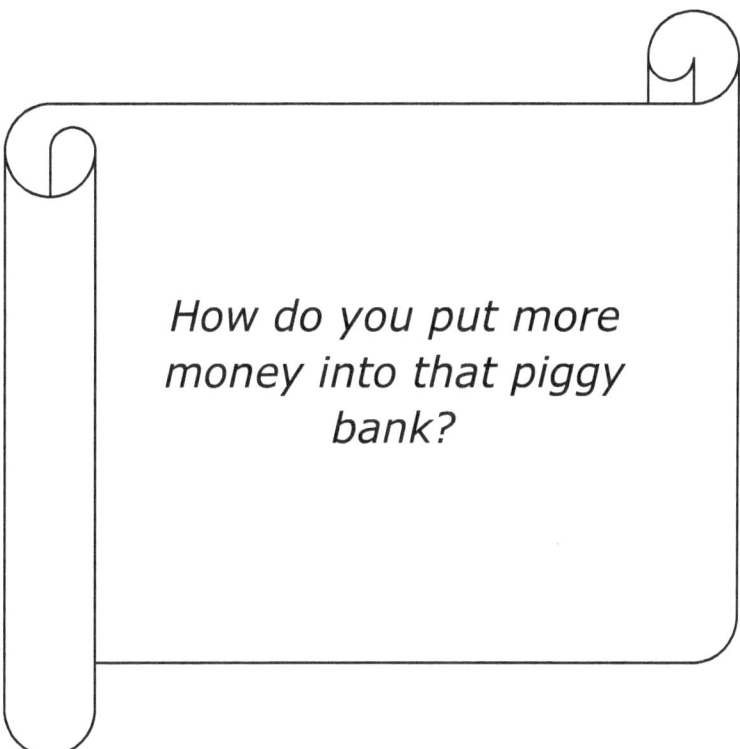

How do you put more money into that piggy bank?

You are adding a bank account or starting your first investment taking the following aspects as a reference.

First, look for the best mentor you can have, don't just grab anyone there, people who are trained and qualified; that responsibly offers that term of investments, achieving better sources of income.

If you have a job, the time has come to invest, to use those investment technologies for cryptocurrencies, for example, let's say that it is the simplest part within the difficult and complex part of investments, because you can invest from a little and thus go up, don't leave that for 10 or 20 years; It is the time now because many of the jobs you are going to start.

In a couple of years to pay with cryptocurrencies and it is time to learn, so October is a perfect time to train yourself in this area, many look for official sources of information that nourish you, I always recommend in this regard, that you inform well, Never make an investment without knowledge.

This is not an investment recommendation, it is knowing that before any action where your money is involved, you should always have prior knowledge of investments.

You are already obtaining better income, it is time to invest and double what you have but with training, through courses, workshops, conferences and trained people.

Do not believe any guru out there who grows overnight, it is my responsibility to explain to you that do not believe just anyone, look for the references of those people, use Google, if they are known or not, look for their professional reference, search an academy that trains you in that aspect.

As I tell you, it is a step that is gradually being created, but it is necessary that I place it there as a great challenge for this year so that it does not go unnoticed within the work and personal well-being that you are creating.

***

Mind Map No. 10

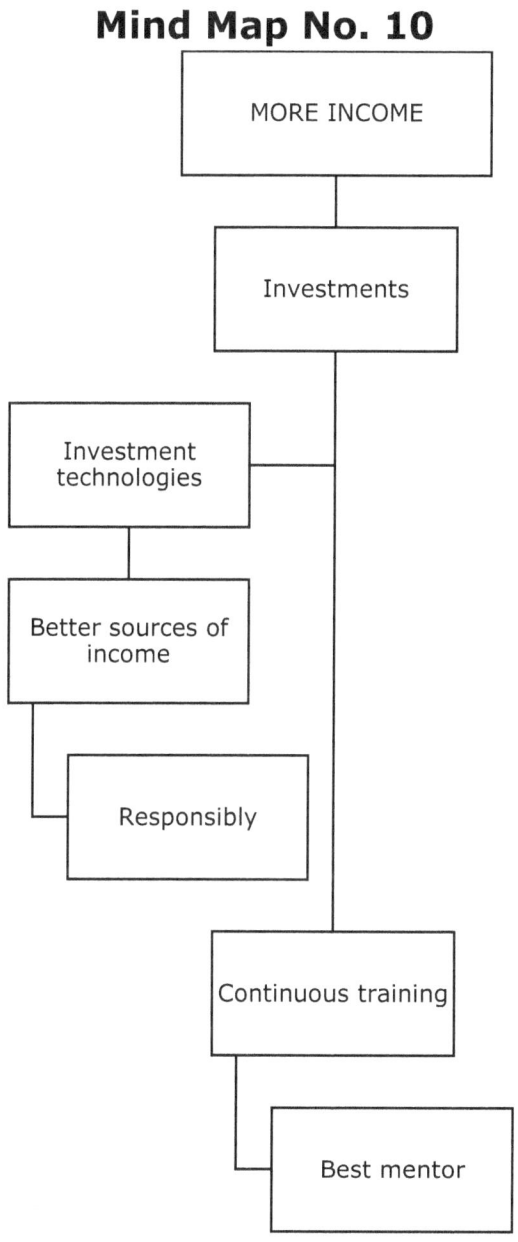

MORE INCOME

Investments

Investment technologies

Better sources of income

Responsibly

Continuous training

Best mentor

Your Mind Map No. 10

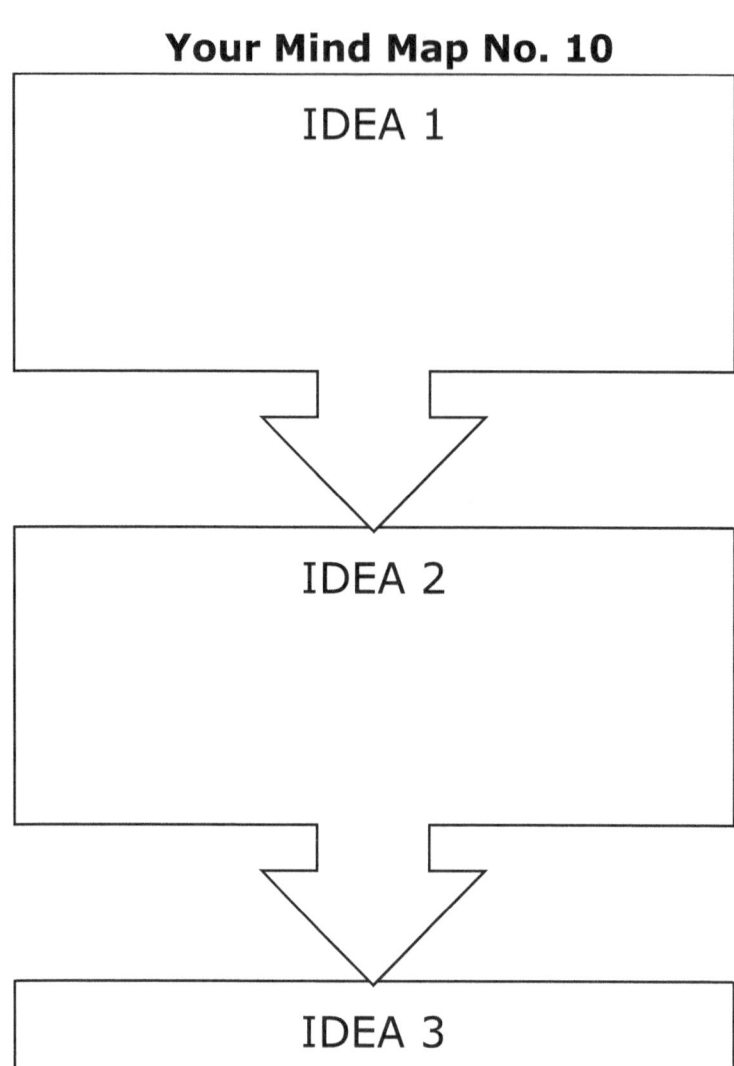

IDEA 1

IDEA 2

IDEA 3

ELEVENTH SECRET

BUILD ON SOLID ROCKS

To be trained in the month of NOVEMBER

CHAPTER XI
Eleventh Secret

You have already been creating this therapy of adaptability and flexibility through values, that self-love that you project in your professional life, but it is time to build on solid rocks, something new, something you are about to create that you can later impact others.

You are going to start building if it is not a business, a job for your own benefit and I am not talking about getting a job but rather something of your own, something that you will leave for your generations, you want to build a new house, build a new garden, build something that will I leave my children to my generations; If you don't have children, increase your efforts, here you want to leave human beings a legacy in this life.

We were not born to come to suffer into the world to cry to become bitter, we came to be happy and what better way is to leave a legacy the moment we leave this life.

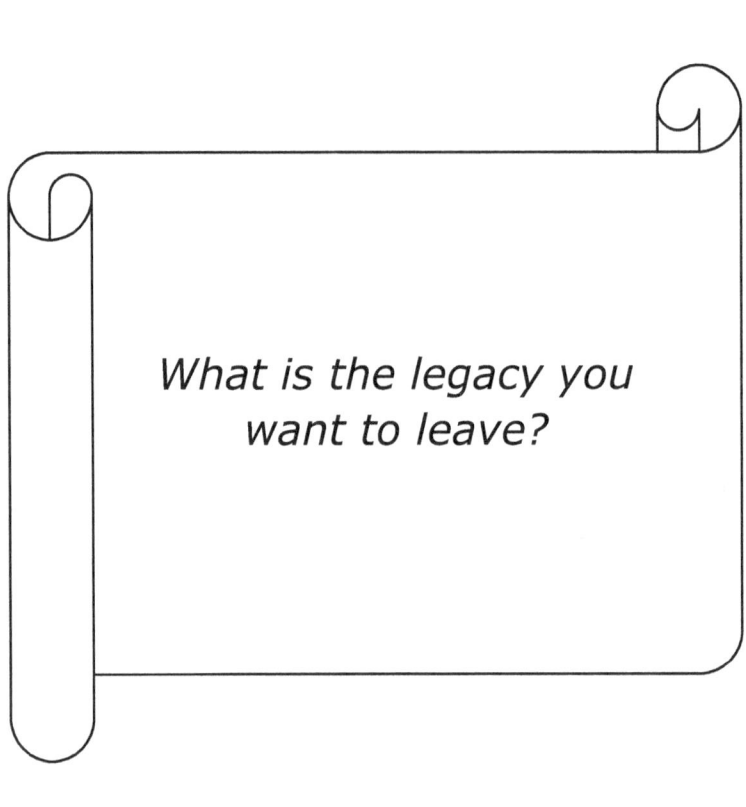

What is the legacy you want to leave?

Let it have strong foundations like a strong rock, let nothing destroy it, build something that no matter how small it may be. Planting a plant, a small tree, that in 20 years will be gigantic is leaving a legacy.

The sea is full of every drop of water and is forming a gigantic one, likewise the tree, that plant that you had the generosity of giving to the environment in this month of November will remain; It will give life to other people through that oxygen that they will breathe. It is the way you leave something solid, even if a hurricane comes that destroys almost everything, but very possibly those roots will still be there and grow back into a very large tree.

With this idea, with this initiative I leave you these reflections, what is your legacy on solid rocks that you are leaving in this month of November as the great challenge.

***

Mind Map No. 11

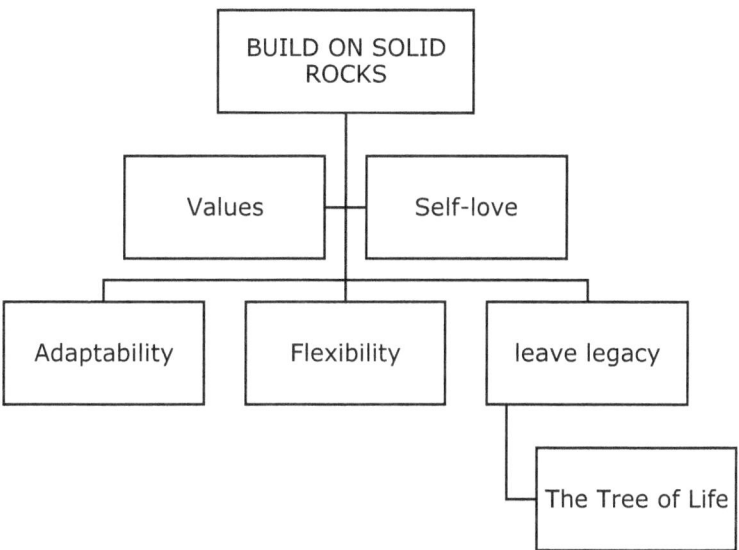

IDEA 1

IDEA 2

IDEA 3

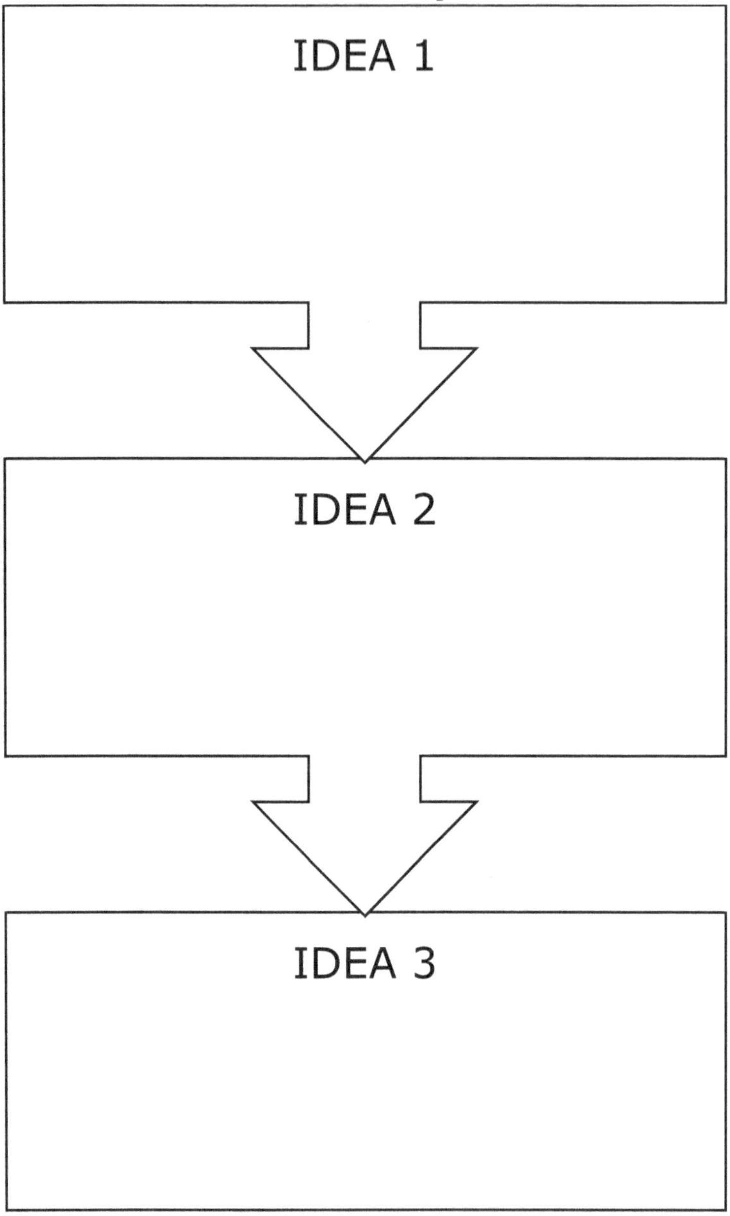

TWELFTH SECRET

REUNION

To be trained in the month of DECEMBER

CHAPTER XII
Twelfth Secret

The reunion of all these months reaches its maximum splendor since December is the month where the most experiences are shown, where we cry, we remember what we did, what we stopped doing, what we want to do.

We set goals but we simply have to let it flow.

*How do you impact others
through your work?*

You have been privately developing this great challenge, which is what you are going to leave to others, as well as the legacy, you project it during the month of December.

What specific activity are you going to do that benefits others in terms of sensitivity and love for nature, for those most in need?

For the child who does not have shoes, for the grandmother who abandoned her, the grandchildren and her other relatives abandoned her in a nursing home.

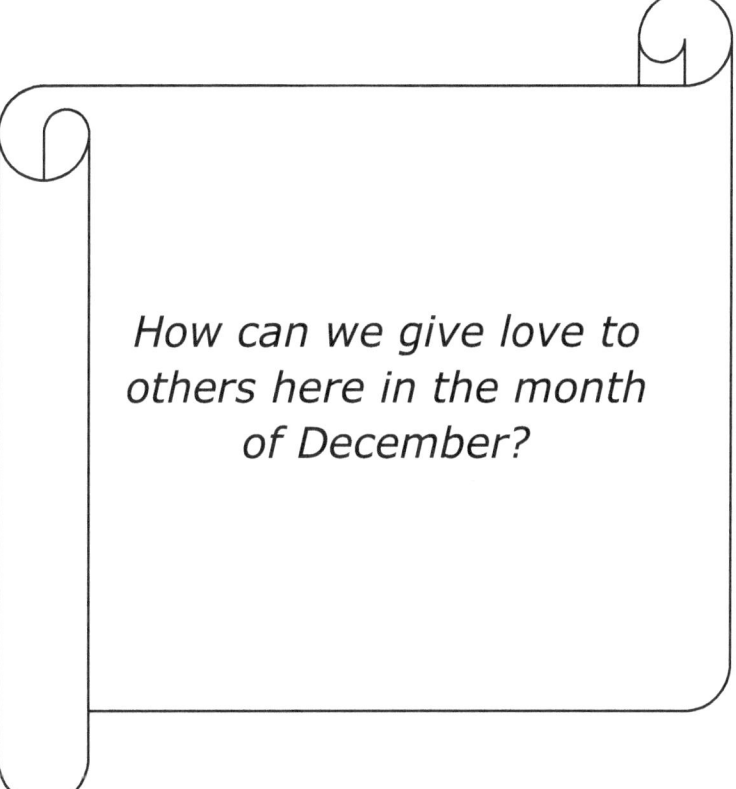

How can we give love to others here in the month of December?

It is to enliven our spirit of altruism and solid solidarity through kindness, generosity, power.

How can you flourish already has come with an extraordinary year through commitment to responsibility to yourself?

In December, project that love towards others, bring them sweet gifts, within your own needs, within your own limitations.

Don't want to donate to children in India if you live in Latin America, it's about where you live and love for others; During December, the month to share and reunite, if the family is at a distance, it is very far away because it is time to strengthen and revive ties.

If you want to give to unknown people, it is a time to donate what you have and turn it around, to turn, activate that energy and that love from you to others.

***

Mind Map No. 12

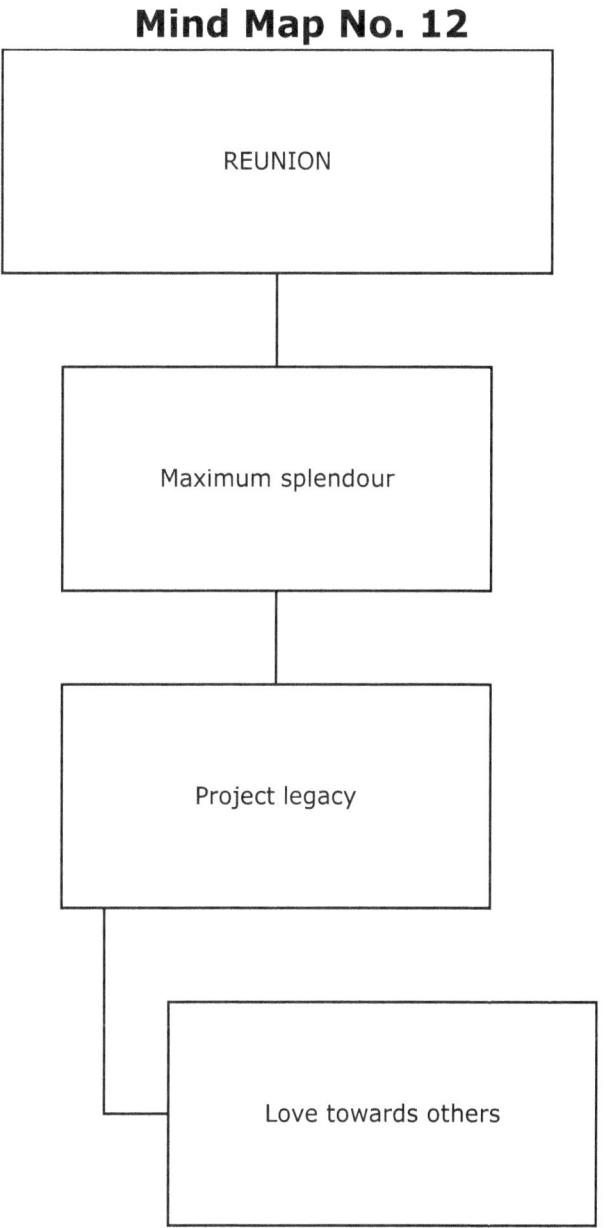

REUNION

Maximum splendour

Project legacy

Love towards others

Your Mind Map No. 12

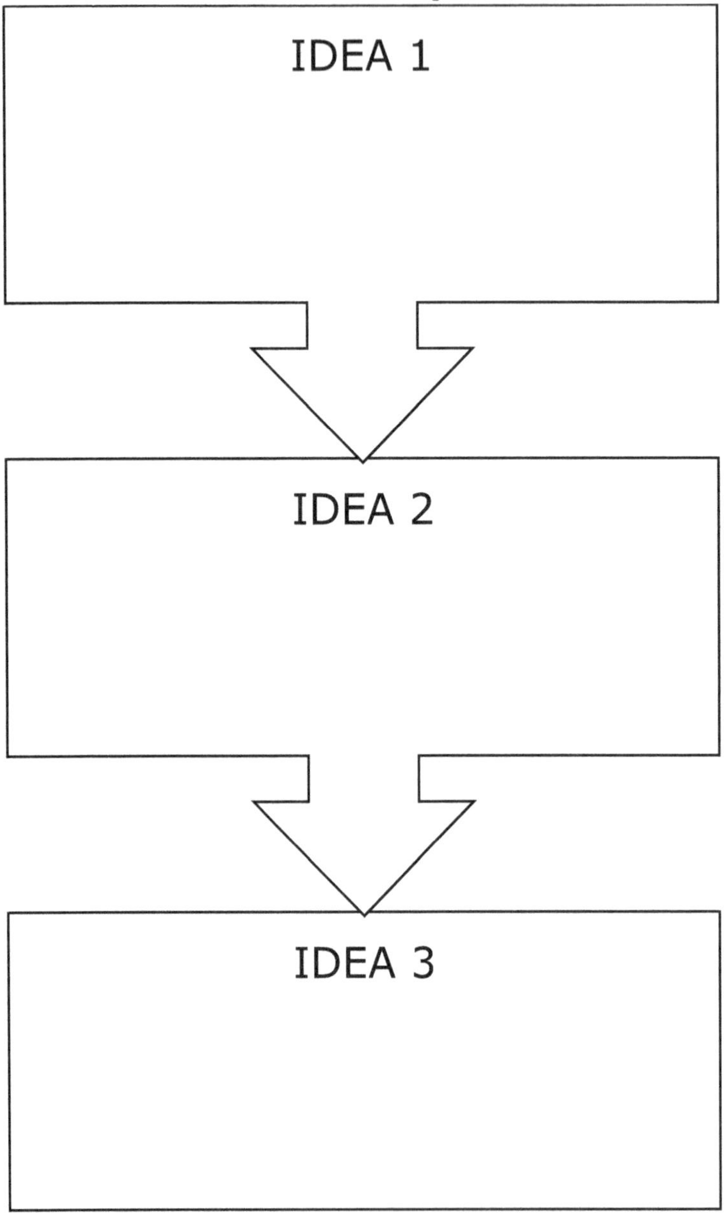

IDEA 1

IDEA 2

IDEA 3

REFLECTIONS OF THE AUTHOR

Finally, I want to thank you for coming this far, because it fills me with great satisfaction that you took your professional training, your personal and work changes seriously.

Commitment, as you read from the beginning, begins with you, in this training as a leader, personally taking the lead in your favor; Obstacles will always arise but every time you feel a decline I want to bring you back to these 12 Challenges of Human Resources as a Great Challenge, because your gifts, that vision of life, will be forceful during all these 12 months and again you will put them into practice, practice.

My invitation has always been to take a pencil and paper, internalize what I have learned, and always put it into practice.

I'm going to give you another great challenge because I always like you to give your neurons mental stimulation so that you continue working.

What would you add additionally to what I am telling you about the 12 Challenges of Human Resources as a great challenge in personal and work life?

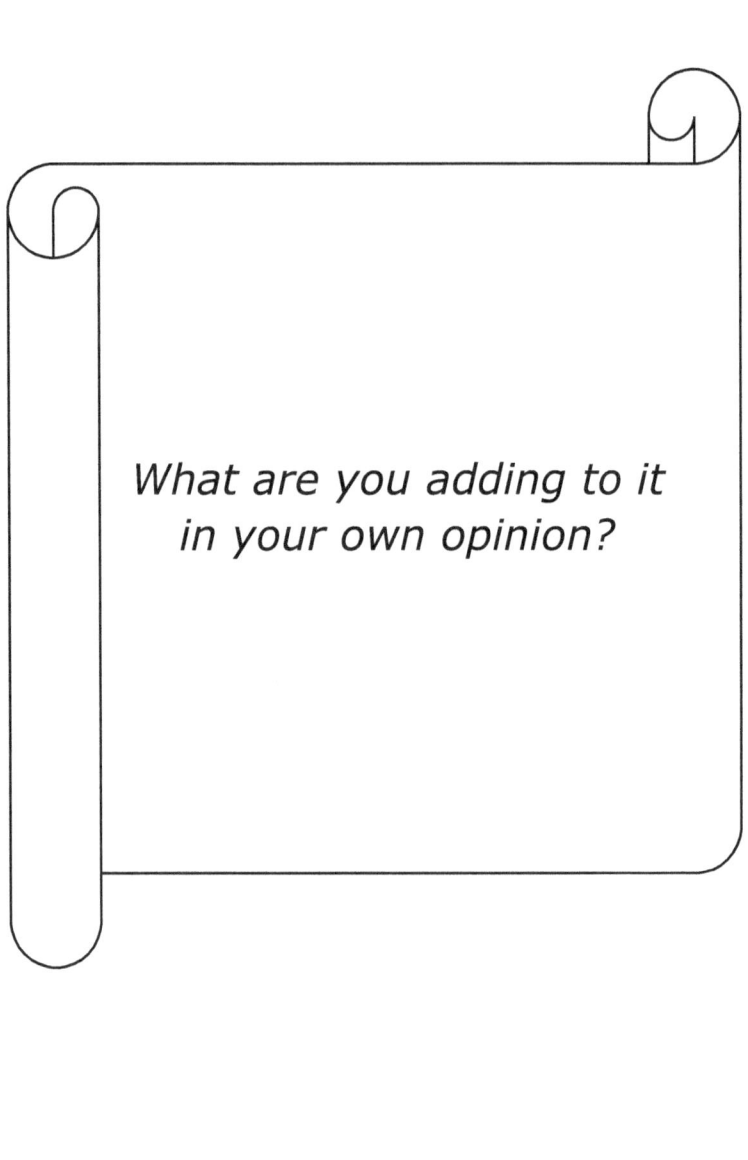

What are you adding to it in your own opinion?

I give you some clues, for many people, they will begin to rotate, leading.

"I prefer that what you told me in October go to January, I prefer that what you told me in March go to the end of the year because my priority is this."

My intention and your actions are for you to break that mold.

What is your great life challenge?

Thank you on behalf of this book for being my reader, for inspiring me to continue writing in this Human Resources Series, I thank you from the bottom of my heart.

Share what you have learned and comment on social networks.

I always read my readers, 100% in all my books and educational programs, I leave you a gift and it is the workbook, take advantage of it and come back here every time you need it to continue building your personal and work well-being. Thank you again Thank you my beloved reader. Thank you for being here and enjoying these 12 Secrets and Challenges of Human Resources.

Post a video of everything you learned in this book on your social networks and tag me #MarbellaMoyaOchoa

***

WORK NOTEBOOK

The workbook below contains three parts of main and supporting ideas that you will need to complete. It is also gridded to stimulate imagination and creativity, use it with complete freedom and thus you will strengthen your brilliant mind.

Main idea 1

Secondary idea 1

Main idea 2

Secondary idea 2

Main idea 3

Secondary idea 3

READER'S REFLECTIONS

Reader's Reflections is an innovation so that the person can reason what they have read and put it into practice.

From a series of questions about the entire content of the book, the reader can respond according to his or her own criteria, making the reading go beyond the traditional because learning is reinforced and places the reader as an active participant in each written word, generating a inseparable interaction between writer and reader.

This relationship is dynamism, to the extent that reading is greatly reinforced and motivates us to transform our world from the static to the mobile, because the reading of any book is the movement of ideas and ultimately the reader's reflections complement people's intellect.

According to what you read, what do the 12 Challenges mean to you?

The different powers are not static. How do you apply these 12 challenges to society?

_____

_____

_____

_____

_____

_____

_____

_____

_____

_____

How do you think these secrets apply on the world stage?

How would what you learned in this book
be applied in society for your learning?

_____

_____

_____

_____

_____

_____

_____

_____

_____

_____

What changes in management learning and work practices should exist today?

INTELLECTUAL AUTOBIOGRAPHY

WRITER

POLITHOLOGIST

ADMINISTRATOR

I was born in the city of Caracas in Venezuela. Professional in Political Science and Administration with more than 13 years of experience. Human Rights Specialist.

I am a multifaceted woman as a writer, Political Scientist and Administrator, inveterate Entrepreneur and Human Resources Mentor by conviction.

Graduated in 2010 with a degree in Political and Administrative Sciences from the Central University of Venezuela, with a mention in Political Science. Simultaneously, I obtained a Bachelor's degree in Administration with a mention in Material and Financial Resources from the Simón Rodríguez National Experimental University. In both within the top 10 of the promotion.

Since 2018, I have assumed the commitment to be CEO – President of the Educando Para La Paz FEPAZ WORLD Foundation, promoting a culture of peace in the human rights of children and families that builds fraternal coexistence without exclusion.

In the same year, she ventured as a freelance writer for Amazon.com, Inc. or its affiliates.

In 2020, Amazon.com, Inc. or its subsidiaries, granted me Amazon Influencer recognition on social networks and through them I teach about the political, social and economic reality of countries, from the human perspective, focusing on working for a world better for love of childhood.

In 2022, I will promote FEPAZ World Academy to more than 100,000 students from 135 countries.

In 2023, the Human Resources Academy and Consultant – ARH International began, to promote the personal and work well-being of people in an innovative and exponential way. In the same year I started the Human Rights Academy – ADH International.

As outstanding features, I am academically trained in Politics,

Administration, Economics, Statistics, Psychology, Philosophy, History, Sociology, International Relations and Law, to observe the environment in a global, critical and objective manner.

BOOKS PUBLISHED ON AMAZON.COM, INC. OR ITS AFFILIATES.

Human Resources Series

HUMAN RESOURCES
Volume I Agile Skills:
Become an expert in leadership and developing high-performance teams.

HUMAN RESOURCES
Volume II Professional Challenges:
Learn the art of leading effective teams.

HUMAN RESOURCES
Volume III Talent Management in the Digital Age:
Develop high-impact business strategies.

- ***My social networks: Marbella Moya Ochoa***
  @mymarbellaochoa

- ***Email: mymarbellaochoa@gmail.com***

- To see more of any series visit my store on Amazon:
  https://www.amazon.com/shop/mymarbellaochoa

- Author page on Amazon:
  https://www.amazon.com/author/mymarbellaochoa

The publication of this work was carried out by:
Marbella Yeniree Moya Ochoa.
Independently published on Amazon.com, Inc. or its affiliates.
This work was published on June 25, 2023.
In Caracas – Venezuela.